Rabbi Nosson Scherman / Rabbi Gedaliah Zlotowitz
General Editors
Rabbi Meir Zlotowitz זצ״ל, *Founder*

ArtScroll® Series

BISTRITZKY EDITION

סדר
השכמת
הבוקר

מודה אני־ברכות השחר

through commentary, stories, and inspiration

Published by

ARTSCROLL
Mesorah Publications, ltd

Arise
and
Sing

The power of the first prayers of the day

YISROEL BESSER

FIRST EDITION
First Impression … November 2021

Published and Distributed by
MESORAH PUBLICATIONS, LTD.
313 Regina Avenue / Rahway, N.J. 07065

Distributed in Europe by
LEHMANNS
Unit E, Viking Business Park
Rolling Mill Road
Jarrow, Tyne & Wear NE32 3DP
England

Distributed in Australia & New Zealand by
GOLDS WORLD OF JUDAICA
3-13 William Street
Balaclava, Melbourne 3183
Victoria Australia

Distributed in Israel by
SIFRIATI / A. GITLER — BOOKS
POB 2351
Bnei Brak 51122

Distributed in South Africa by
KOLLEL BOOKSHOP
Northfield centre, 17 Northfield Avenue
Glenhazel 2192, Johannesburg, South Africa

ARTSCROLL® SERIES
ARISE AND SING
© Copyright 2021, by MESORAH PUBLICATIONS, Ltd.
313 Regina Avenue / Rahway, N.J. 07065 / (718) 921-9000 / www.artscroll.com

---

ITEM CODE: ARISH
ISBN 10: 1-4226-3006-4
ISBN 13: 978-1-4226-3006-8

Typography by CompuScribe at ArtScroll Studios, Ltd.

Printed in the United States of America.
Bound by Sefercraft, Quality Bookbinders, Ltd., Rahway NJ

*W*ith reverence for their *kiddush Hashem*
we humbly dedicate this volume to
the memory of the six million *kedoshim* הי״ד.
Their holy imprint lives forever.

Generations have risen since, but the awe at how
they lived — and how they died — only grows.

The theme of this volume, "*Modeh Ani ...
shehechezarta bi nishmasi*, We thank You ... for
You have restored us to life," has been realized in
our nation. We were given the privilege and the
blessings to rebuild, standing tall and proud.

It is to them, the *kedoshim*, in whose holy footsteps we
walk, and whose legacy lights our way, that we dedicate
this volume in gratitude to Hashem for His blessings,
and the opportunities He gives us each new day.

ת.נ.צ.ב.ה.

Joseph and Sheila Bistritzky
and family

ஃ Table of Contents ௸

✍ Introduction ✍

Not long after we emerged from the lockdown of the spring of 2020, I was speaking with my friend and mentor, Rabbi Gedaliah Zlotowitz.

People, it turned out, enjoyed davening. Several months of davening at home, three *tefillos* a day, with nowhere to rush to — offices closed, stores shuttered, no carpools or appointments — gave them time to daven slowly, to ponder each word.

The sense of panic and urgency in the streets made each word of *tefillah* a lifeline, every phrase of longing a raft to grasp tightly in an ocean of fear.

And then, *b'chasdei Hashem*, the world began reopening, people back to shul, back to work, back to the rush, rush, rush of everyday life, and davening once again was something else that had to get done. *I can make the 7:30 minyan if I hurry.*

Would the sweet sense of total immersion in *tefillah* disappear?

For the *mispallelim*, those who learn *sifrei avodah*, who invest time and heart in each *tefillah*, perhaps the danger presented by this lost opportunity is slim, but what about the rest of us?

Reb Gedaliah, ever-attuned to spiritual opportunities, had the idea to take various segments of *tefillah* and present them with context, a mix of commentary and inspiration.

We started with *Nishmas*, last winter, and the response validated his sense that people wanted to connect to *tefillah* on a deeper level. With Hashem's help, we move to *Birchos HaShachar*, the prayers offered during first few moments of the new day: in a sense, the keys that will unlock all the blessing the day has to offer. Like anything with great potential, it's easy to miss the chance to make the most of these moments, the words mumbled while rushing, rushing, rushing.

Not just gratitude, but such vital requests as well!

Rav Zev Binder (Zev Avrohom ben Yosef Shalom) was a beloved and respected *maggid shiur* in the Yeshiva Gedolah of Montreal. He was *niftar* suddenly, very suddenly, plunging his family, *talmidim,* and an entire community into mourning.

Not long after his *petirah*, I was writing a tribute article to him, and one of his children shared something profound. Their family had made the drive from Lakewood to Montreal overnight, arriving just as dawn broke: unsure about their halachic eligibility to say the morning *berachos*, since they hadn't slept very much, they asked Reb Zev to be *motzi* them with the *berachos*.

He was clearly hesitant, so they asked someone else to say the *berachos*. Later, one of the children asked their father, who was generally so amenable and happy to do a favor, why he appeared reluctant to accommodate that particular request.

Reb Zev explained that his schedule was quite busy: he did not always have the luxury of davening for his own success in Torah, for that of his children and their children, for all the children of Klal Yisrael, the way he would have liked to.

"And so it is, then, early each morning, when I say the *Birchos HaTorah*, that I have the chance to really daven. It's a very special time, and also a private time, so I wasn't so comfortable giving it up if there were other options."

Those who see past the façade, the distraction and noise of this world, appreciate the first minutes of the new day for another reason as well.

The world is still, pure, the soul sanctified by its brush with the heavens, and even this world appears tinged with holiness.

Those whose vision is fine-tuned to all aspects of *kedushah* hold onto that feeling well into the day, unwilling to relinquish the purity, the luminescence, the spiritual sparkle of morning.

A *talmid* recalled accompanying Rav Moshe Shapira on a visit to England. They were at the airport for the return flight, standing amid typical Heathrow bedlam, blaring loudspeakers and rushing porters, frantic passengers and overwhelmed agents. As they waited to board, the commotion increased. And Reb Moshe was humming to himself.

The *talmid* listened. His rebbi was softly singing an ancient *piyut*, "Odeh LaKeil Leivav Choker," recited by some people at daybreak.

I thank the God Who probes all hearts, when stars sing in the morning.

Simu lev el haneshamah.

Pay heed to your own soul, opal, amethyst, and gold,

As bright as is the sun's warm glow, far brighter than the morning!

MiKisei Kavod chutzavah.

From under the Throne of Glory she is hewn, to roam this wilderness,

To redeem us from wrath's flame, and light our way before morning.

It is a poetic call to the soul to remember from whence the soul comes, and for what purpose it has come down to earth. The song tells of the *neshamah*'s journey from the spheres of holiness down to a harsh world. It's a reminder that each night, the soul rises to give an accounting of its deeds, and it describes the joy of a soul that arises "resplendent, in a *tallis* and *tefillin*, splendid as an ornamented bride..."

Reb Moshe, his *talmid* understood, was rising above it all, the bustle and activity and sheer earthliness of it — connecting himself with the world beyond.

Reb Moshe hummed to himself as he walked down the walkway and onto the plane, still there, the world bright and clean, singing the song of the morning-star.

That, then, is the hope of this *sefer*: perhaps we will be

able not only to appreciate these moments more, but also to develop eyes to see morning, to see the renewal, the world's rebirth, and that way, be a bit more connected with the One Who in His goodness every day perpetually renews the work of Creation.

This book owes its existence to the vision and guidance of Rabbi Gedaliah Zlotowitz. Every book with the ArtScroll imprint is stamped with the *seichel*, perceptiveness and wisdom, of Rabbi Nosson Scherman, fused with the precision and style of Rabbi Sheah Brander.

This manuscript has benefited greatly from the magic red pen of Mrs. Judi Dick, and has been enhanced by the ever-innovative Reb Eli Kroen, who keeps raising his own high bar. Rabbi Avrohom Biderman is a cherished friend and sounding board, Rabbi Mendy Herzberg manages to somehow juggle deadlines and word counts and a million other details while smiling, and Mrs. Estie Dicker takes unfinished work and seals it with the touch of excellence. Mrs. Mindy Stern and Mrs. Esther Feierstein proofread, ensuring that this book meet the high standards of an ArtScroll book. Chanie Ziegler did a masterful job with the finishing touches. Rabbi Ahron Zlotowitz is a dear friend whose advice and insight are always on the mark, and Rabbi Yitzchak Hisiger brings a welcome dose of positive energy to any project. The ArtScroll production floor is a symphony of sophisticated machinery singing the song of *harbatzas Torah*. The conductor of that symphony is Moshe Scheinbaum, whose enthusiasm for his work radiates throughout the massive room.

My gratitude for being part of this team is profound.

I drew on many *sefarim* and books while working on this. I am particularly grateful for the insights of Rav Yitzchak Sender in the Commentator's Siddur, and to Reb Michael Rothschild for the very helpful *sefarim* he recommended.

Modeh ani lefanecha...for those who surround me, the people in my own life fill me with appreciation. My rebbeim, who walk me down roads of clarity and encouragement, and our grandparents, lighthouses of guidance, inspiration, and *tefillah.* Our parents are treasure-troves of love, care, and unwavering loyalty, steady and sure at each juncture.

My wife and children are the bright rays of sun shining into my own life, each one a blessing. I am grateful to a life's partner who inspires and encourages me at every moment, and for the *nachas* and joy we experience each day.

May it keep increasing.

וְנִהְיֶה אֲנַחְנוּ וְצֶאֱצָאֵינוּ וְצֶאֱצָאֵי צֶאֱצָאֵינוּ וְצֶאֱצָאֵי עַמְּךָ בֵּית יִשְׂרָאֵל כֻּלָּנוּ
יוֹדְעֵי שְׁמֶךָ וְלוֹמְדֵי תוֹרָתֶךָ לִשְׁמָהּ

Yisroel Besser

Aseres Yemei Teshuvah, 5782

ᔯ Appreciating Berachah ᔰ

The *Nefesh HaChaim* quotes the *Zohar HaKadosh* on the *pasuk, Give strength to Hashem* (*Tehillim* 68:35), by addressing the question: How can mere mortals give strength to the Creator? The *Zohar HaKadosh* explains that prosecuting angels complain and find fault with the actions of the Jews, hoping to generate judgment in the world. This, in effect, is an "attack" on Hakadosh Baruch Hu, Who wants only to shower blessing on His children. Through our actions, then, we are able to strengthen Hashem, allowing Him to overcome the arguments of the prosecutors.

This is true with every mitzvah, but when we recite a *berachah*, we are giving strength to "blessing" Hashem, asking that the flow of His goodness and strength increase in our world.

> *I would like to explain the meaning of* בָּרוּךְ אַתָּה ה', *with which we begin all of our berachos. The word baruch is usually translated to mean "blessed." The concept of "blessing Hakadosh Baruch Hu" must be understood. How can we, mere mortals, give our sanction to the Borei Olam, as if we had the power to affect Him through our words of blessing? For this reason, some of the mefarshei hatefillah explain Baruch Atah to mean, "You are the source of all blessings." However, this still leaves unexplained*

*certain usages, such as "I shall bless Hashem" (ibid.
34:2), "But we will bless God" (ibid. 115:18), and
other similar pesukim.*

*We therefore think that the sense in which the
word baruch is used in our berachos is that of ribui,
meaning to add, to increase. For instance, "He will
increase your bread and your water" (Shemos 23:25).
It is in this sense that we say to Hakadosh Baruch
Hu as an introduction to every berachah: It is our
tefillah that You may be increasingly recognized in
the world: by our own personal, enhanced emunah,
and also by the world at large, so that more and more
people will live their lives according to Your will.*

(*Rav Schwab on Prayer*, ArtScroll/Mesorah)

In this vein, Rabbeinu Bachya explains that the word *bera-chah* is connected with that of *bereichah*, a wellspring that flows from the ground, water rushing forward without limit.

The word *berachah* itself indicates that it is an expression of increase, reveals the Maharal (*Tiferes Yisrael* 34), since the letters ב, ר, and כ all have something in common. The *gematria* of each letter represents a doubling of the letter before it: ב doubling one, כ doubling ten, and ר doubling 100. This hints at the power of a *berachah* to bring additional, increased good into the world.

As we start a new day by reciting the *Birchos HaShachar*, we take a moment to contemplate not just the awesome power in what we're about to say, but the obvious power of man, crown of creation, who is given the merit and privilege of blessing the King of kings and, with each word, affecting the entire universe.

סדר השכמת הבוקר
מודה אני־ברכות השחר

Arise *and* Sing

יִתְגַּבֵּר כָּאֲרִי לַעֲמוֹד בַּבּוֹקֶר לַעֲבוֹדַת בּוֹרְאוֹ

One should strengthen himself in the morning to arise like a lion to serve the Creator.

—————————————————— *Shulchan Aruch 1:1*

These are the opening words to the complete code of how a Jew conducts his life. Why are these the opening words to the entire *Shulchan Aruch*?

The commentaries teach that the way we wake up reflects our attitude not just toward the day but toward the night's sleep as well. Sleep is not just an escape, and we weren't merely unconscious — the sleep itself had meaning. In those hours of slumber, our bodies received much-needed rest. Our bodies, physical homes to our souls, are our partners in serving Hashem. Sleep is important; in proclaiming, through the way we wake up, that we are soldiers, ready to serve, we are asserting that there is importance and value to our sleep.

Why as a lion? Because the lion is marked not just by its majesty and strength, but by its fearlessness.

And from the moment a person is awake, the *yetzer hara* is right there, hard at work seeking to get him to slip or stumble.

But we are poised like a lion, unafraid of the challenges that lie ahead, for to struggle is to be alive and we are ready.

The term *yisgaber*, to strengthen oneself, has a message of its own, the Ben Ish Chai explains: the recognition that being alive means being tempted by the *yetzer hara*. It is an integral part of life; the *yetzer hara* is always right there, trying to overwhelm a person and defeat him. It takes strength and focus, but if you proclaim loud and clear, at the very start of the day, that you are not afraid, you have established a winning pattern.

❧◈❧

Upon arising, a person should recite Modeh Ani immediately, even before washing his hands. We begin the day by contemplating Hashem's kindness in restoring our souls to us, allowing us to begin a new day, filled with promise, feeling refreshed.

מוֹדֶה אֲנִי לְפָנֶיךָ, מֶלֶךְ חַי וְקַיָם, שֶׁהֶחֱזַרְתָּ בִּי נִשְׁמָתִי בְּחֶמְלָה — רַבָּה אֱמוּנָתֶךָ.

מוֹדֶה אֲנִי לְפָנֶיךָ, מֶלֶךְ חַי וְקַיָם
— שֶׁהֶחֱזַרְתָּ בִּי נִשְׁמָתִי בְּחֶמְלָה, רַבָּה אֱמוּנָתֶךָ
I gratefully thank You, O living and eternal King,
for You have returned my soul within me with
compassion — abundant is Your faithfulness!

From the first moments of a new day, we are aware, we are connected, and we are filled with gratitude. Why do greet the new day specifically with these words?

There are those who suggest that since it is forbidden to utter words of holiness before washing one's hands, this *tefillah*, which does not mention the Name of Hashem, is a fitting way to start the day.

Perhaps there is another message here as well: gratitude is what makes us who we are. The Chiddushei HaRim teaches that we are referred to as *Yehudim* because our defining characteristic is that of *hoda'ah*, acknowledgment, the awareness that we are beholden to our Creator. As we awaken, the sun rising on a new day, we are immediately "*modeh.*"

— מֶלֶךְ חַי וְקַיָם
O living and eternal King.

Even the supposedly great superpowers of the world, rulers and leaders, are transient in nature. They appear to be invincible, but they eventually fade away and disappear. But ever since Avraham Avinu discovered the existence of our Creator, parents have transmitted this truth to their children, imbuing them with a knowledge of a King Who is not just powerful, but alive and eternal.

ᘯ Upon Arising ᘰ

I gratefully thank You, O living and eternal King, for You have returned my soul within me with compassion — abundant is Your faithfulness!

רַבָּה אֱמוּנָתֶךָ —
Abundant is Your faithfulness!

It was morning in Siberia, and in a freezing hut, a recent arrival began a new day.

Rav Yechezkel Abramsky, accustomed to addressing his Father in Heaven directly, lifted his gaze toward the heavens and spoke.

"Dear Father," he said, "here I am, on my first day in the wasteland of Siberia, because this is where You, dear Father, want me to be. But Tatte, I have nothing here, none of my precious sefarim from which to learn, no clothing to keep me warm in the freezing climate, so with what can I start this day? How do I say 'Modeh Ani' on this day? For what do I thank You?"

And in a voice filled with enthusiasm, the Rav continued.

"There is something I have with me, a gift that no one can take away, ever.

"My emunah, my faith in You and the precision of Your plan, dear Father. That's right here, inside me now, as always. And for that, Tatte, I say thank You… so Modeh ani… for this fact, that 'rabbah emunasecha,' my emunah is great and limitless, always with me. For this, I am so grateful."

(When Rav Yosef Yitzchok Schneerson of Lubavitch heard this thought from Rav Abramsky, the Rebbe — himself a survivor of Russian brutality and harassment — grew emotional. "All that you endured," the Rebbe said, "was worth it so that you merited to say this *vort*, to develop this thought.")

Thank You for our *emunah*: because this is part of us always, the flame of faith burning bright.

רַבָּה אֱמוּנָתֶךְ —
Abundant is Your faithfulness!

How does Hashem show His faithfulness?

The words *rabbah emunasecha* refer to Hashem's faithfulness, the *emunah* that He possesses.[1] What does this mean, that the Master of the universe believes? Why would He Who knows what the future holds require faith?

The answer is right here. Each night, the soul goes up to Heaven, judged anew. We know the truth. Maybe we could have been better or done more. Maybe today wasn't perfect...

But then we open our eyes and we realize that He has given us back our souls, refreshed and invigorated and ready to fulfill our mission yet again, and we realize...

Rabbah emunasecha! Great is His faithfulness in us!

He believes in us, trusts that today we will do better, today we will justify His never-ending confidence in us. By restoring our souls, He indicates that we are up to the task.

And with this foundation, we are ready to face the day ahead!

מוֹדֶה אֲנִי —
I gratefully thank You.

Why, when we recite the Thirteen Principles of Faith, at the end of Shacharis, do we start each one by saying, "*Ani maamin,* I believe," yet here we say "*Modeh ani,*" in the reverse order? Why not "*Ani modeh*"?

---

1. Based on the *pasuk,* חֲדָשִׁים לַבְּקָרִים רַבָּה אֱמוּנָתֶךְ, *They are new every morning, great is Your faithfulness* (Eichah 3:23).

By using the word "*ani*," one is making a statement. *Ani* is a declaration that I exist, I am present.

After *tefillas Shacharis* — once the Jew has prayed, perhaps donned *tefillin* or *tallis*, connected with the Creator — his existence has been defined. However, when he begins the day, before he utters words of *tefillah*, he is a creature not yet stamped with purpose. Therefore, first he is *modeh*, expressing gratitude, and that itself transforms him into an "*ani*." A Jew's existence emanates from his recognition that there is a Creator to Whom he is grateful.

מֶלֶךְ חַי וְקַיָּם —
O living and eternal King.

As we thank Hashem for restoring our *neshamos,* we express gratitude for the fact that the One giving us back our souls is a King Who is "living and eternal," with the power to renew and refresh the *neshamah*. We aren't merely being granted yesterday's soul, but rather, a soul safeguarded by and granted once more by the Source of life Himself. He is "*chai vekayam,* living and eternal," and He has imbued in our souls a spark of the Divine, those very same properties.

מוֹדֶה אֲנִי לְפָנֶיךָ, מֶלֶךְ חַי וְקַיָּם,
שֶׁהֶחֱזַרְתָּ בִּי נִשְׁמָתִי בְּחֶמְלָה, רַבָּה אֱמוּנָתֶךָ —
I gratefully thank You, O living and eternal King,
for You have returned my soul within me with
compassion — abundant is Your faithfulness!

Chazal teach that Dovid HaMelech would sleep less than sixty breaths at a time. The *Mechaber* (*Orach Chaim* 4:16) cites this and explains that it was כְּדֵי שֶׁלֹּא יִטְעוֹם טַעַם מִיתָה, *in order that he not experience the taste of death*. Since sleep is considered to be 1/60 of death, and sixty breaths is considered the minimum for sleep, Dovid avoided sleeping for that length of time.[2]

---

2. See *Beur Halachah* ibid. for a practical discussion regarding the time it takes for sixty breaths.

רֵאשִׁית חָכְמָה יִרְאַת יהוה, שֵׂכֶל טוֹב לְכָל עֹשֵׂיהֶם, תְּהִלָּתוֹ עֹמֶדֶת לָעַד.[1] בָּרוּךְ שֵׁם כְּבוֹד מַלְכוּתוֹ לְעוֹלָם וָעֶד.[2]

And so, perhaps this is why we recite this particular attribute of Hashem when we arise from sleep. Even though we did, in fact, sleep, we are confident that the One Who is Living and Eternal, before Whom there is no sleep, has returned to us a *neshamah* stamped with His life.

בְּחֶמְלָה, רַבָּה אֱמוּנָתֶךָ —
With compassion — abundant is Your faithfulness.

The *Yad Ephraim* points out that there are those who read the final phrase as "*b'chemlah rabbah*" and then conclude with the word "*emunasecha*," gratitude to Hashem for returning our *neshamos* with "great compassion" followed by an expression of faith — but this is a mistake. The phrase is based on the *pasuk,* חֲדָשִׁים לַבְּקָרִים רַבָּה אֱמוּנָתֶךָ, *They are new every morning, great is Your faithfulness* (*Eichah* 3:23), and the correct way to recite it is: שֶׁהֶחֱזַרְתָּ בִּי נִשְׁמָתִי בְּחֶמְלָה, *for You have returned my soul within me with compassion,* after which there is a pause, and then the concluding statement, that רַבָּה אֱמוּנָתֶךָ, *abundant is Your faithfulness.*

שֶׁהֶחֱזַרְתָּ בִּי נִשְׁמָתִי בְּחֶמְלָה — *For You have returned my soul within me with compassion.*

It is possible that a child will run away from school, upset about one thing or another. He will run all the way home as fast he can, promising that he will never return to school again.

The parents will take him by the hand and lead him back to school, intent on making it clear that this is where he belongs and will be most productive.

The beginning of wisdom is the fear of HASHEM, good understanding [is given] to all who practice them; His praise endures forever.[1] *Blessed is the Name of His glorious kingdom for all eternity.*[2]

_____

(1) *Tehillim* 111:10. (2) 104:1-2.

And what does the teacher do when this child is brought back to class? The wise educator will smile broadly and say, "Welcome back, *tzaddik*, we are so happy to have you. We will make sure that things are better for you from now on."

We, too, arise in the morning and joyfully react to the fact that our precious *neshamah* is back within us, there where it, and we, can be most productive. Thank You, we say, for the fact that "You have brought it back to me," given me another chance, and this time, I will make sure that it is utilized properly as well.

רַבָּה אֱמוּנָתֶךָ — *Abundant is Your faithfulness.*

We conclude our opening sentence of the new day with an expression of faith in Hashem, because Chazal teach us that sleep is a taste of death. And now, seeing how the body awakens from the deepest slumber, we are reminded that even when the body rests the ultimate rest, it will also awaken.

From the fact that we awaken each day, we develop new *emunah* in *Techiyas HaMeisim,* the Resurrection of the Dead.

רֵאשִׁית חָכְמָה יִרְאַת ה', שֵׂכֶל טוֹב לְכָל עֹשֵׂיהֶם, תְּהִלָּתוֹ עוֹמֶדֶת לָעַד — *The beginning of wisdom is the fear of Hashem, good understanding [is given] to all who practice them; His praise endures forever.*

This is recited to make it clear that at the outset of the day, we understand that the ultimate goal — the pursuit of wisdom — is attainable only once there is fear of God.

In *Mishlei* (1:7), Rashi states with regard to this *pasuk*:

תּוֹרָה צִוָּה לָנוּ מֹשֶׁה, מוֹרָשָׁה קְהִלַּת
יַעֲקֹב. ³ שְׁמַע בְּנִי מוּסַר אָבִיךָ, וְאַל תִּטֹּשׁ
תּוֹרַת אִמֶּךָ. ⁴ תּוֹרָה תְהֵא אֱמוּנָתִי, וְאֵל
שַׁדַּי בְּעֶזְרָתִי. וְאַתֶּם הַדְּבֵקִים בַּיהוה
אֱלֹהֵיכֶם, חַיִּים כֻּלְּכֶם הַיּוֹם. ⁵ לִישׁוּעָתְךָ
קִוִּיתִי יהוה. ⁶

"Before your wisdom, first fear your Creator, and that will give your heart the desire to engage in wisdom and in knowledge, for the fools, who do not fear the Lord, despise wisdom and discipline."

Throughout the generations, our *gedolei Torah* were celebrated not just for their Torah knowledge, but for their genuine fear of Heaven; the logic and reason of the Torah were dominated by their awe before the One Who gave the Torah.

Rav Moshe Feinstein was once at a hotel, participating in a convention. Someone entered the ballroom looking for him, since he had an important phone call at the front desk. As Rav Moshe was walking out, he passed a *minyan* that had formed in the hallway for Minchah, and one of the *mispallelim* was still davening *Shemoneh Esrei* in his path.

As proscribed by halachah, Rav Moshe stood in place, not walking by the *mispallel*. Long-distance phone calls were expensive in those days and the caller had clearly said that it was very important.

People looked on in surprise as Rav Moshe stood in place, waiting patiently for the man to finish davening — was there not any sort of *heter* that would permit him to slip by? A *talmid* asked the Rosh Yeshivah about it, and Rav Moshe explained.

"*Voss heist*, what do you mean?" he asked. "There was a wall there! If halachah dictates that it's prohibited to pass, then it is not possible to keep walking!"

The Torah that was commanded to us by Moshe is the heritage of the congregation of Yaakov.[3] *Hear, my child, the discipline of your father, and do not forsake the teaching of your mother.*[4] *The Torah should be my faith, and El Shaddai should assist me. But you who cling to Hashem, your God — you are all alive today.*[5] *For Your salvation do I long, O HASHEM!*[6]

---

(3) *Devarim* 33:4. (4) *Mishlei* 1:8. (5) *Devarim* 4:4. (6) *Bereishis* 49:18.

That the essence of the Torah scholar is his fear of Heaven is clear from the Gemara (*Berachos* 58a), says Rav Yitzchok Sorotzkin. There, we are taught: "One who sees the sages of Israel recites: *Blessed… Who has shared of His wisdom with those who revere Him.*"

The defining title for the sages, the great *talmidei chachamim* of Klal Yisrael, is "*yerei'av,*" those who revere Him, because it is in that reverence that their Torah greatness is evident as well. Without pure fear of Heaven, wisdom has little value.

That is the beginning of wisdom, and it is with this that we begin a new day.

תּוֹרָה צִוָּה לָנוּ מֹשֶׁה מוֹרָשָׁה קְהִלַּת יַעֲקֹב —
The Torah that was commanded to us by Moshe is the heritage of the congregation of Yaakov.

The *roshei teivos* (first letters) of the words צִוָּה לָנוּ מֹשֶׁה form the word צֶלֶם, *tzelem,* says the Imrei Emes of Ger, the Divine image in which man was formed. It is the Torah that gives man dimensions of greatness. Torah takes a mere human and makes him a *tzelem Elokim,* capable of impacting events and his own destiny.

It is the Torah and its precepts that give us that sense of worth and power.

Chazal (*Succah* 42a) teach that as soon as a child knows how to speak, his father must teach him words of Torah and the *pasuk* of *Shema Yisrael*.

Which words of Torah are taught to a child? Rav Hamnuna says that this refers to the *pasuk*, תּוֹרָה צִוָּה לָנוּ מֹשֶׁה מוֹרָשָׁה קְהִלַּת יַעֲקֹב, *The Torah that was commanded to us by Moshe is the heritage of the congregation of Yaakov* (*Devarim* 33:4). And what is the *pasuk* taught to a child who has just learned to speak? The Gemara answers: It is referring to the first verse of *Krias Shema* — *Shema Yisrael Hashem Elokeinu Hashem Echad*.

Why these two *pesukim?* Rabbi Moshe Cordovero explains that between them, the essence of Yiddishkeit is reflected: firstly, *Shema Yisrael*, the knowledge that Hashem exists and He is One. And secondly, that the Torah has come from Him, brought down by Moshe Rabbeinu for the benefit of an entire nation.

ﻪﺵ Ahavas Yisrael

The *Magen Avraham* (46) says that a person should accept the mitzvah of *ahavas Yisrael*, to love all Jews, at this time. This *minhag* was instituted by the Arizal, who taught his *talmidim* to recite the words, הֲרֵינִי מְקַבֵּל עָלַי מִצְוַת עֲשֵׂה שֶׁל וְאָהַבְתָּ לְרֵעֲךָ כָּמוֹךָ, *I accept upon myself the positive commandment of "You shall love your friend as yourself,"* before beginning to daven Shacharis. What's the significance of this particular mitzvah before starting a new day's *tefillah?*

The *Kitzur Shulchan Aruch* (12:2) explains. "Unity and connection in the lower realms (represented by *ahavas Yisrael*) create a bond in the higher spheres as well, and the *tefillos* join together and are beloved by Hashem."

Rav Yisroel Dovid Schlesinger connected this with the teaching of the Gemara (*Sotah* 34a) that the weight a person can lift onto his shoulders is one-third of that which he can bear when others place the load on him. Working in sync, people can bear much greater weight, and *tefillos* that are joined together with the *tefillos* of an entire nation or congregation are that much more effective.

Before we start davening, we remind ourselves of our obligations to our fellow Jews, and the ability we have to improve their situation.

Yeshivah Moreshes Yehoshua, founded and led by Rav Dovid Trenk, was running a kesivas Sefer Torah campaign to raise funds for the yeshivah.

The yeshivah office sent out a mailing that included details of the campaign, and options for donors to dedicate different letters and pesukim in the Torah.

One of the askanim involved in the campaign received a phone call from his rebbi, Reb Dovid, but since he was in the middle of an important meeting, he was not able to answer. Reb Dovid called again, and then a third time, but this askan did not answer.

Finally, the doorbell rang, and there was Reb Dovid, unable to wait another moment.

He explained the urgency. "In today's mail, many envelopes came from donors to the Sefer Torah campaign, including one person who asked for the pasuk, אֵל נָא רְפָא נָא לָהּ, 'I beseech you, God, please heal her' (Bamidbar 12:13). You know that I just moved to Lakewood, so I am not yet familiar with the names of the people who live here. I need your help to figure out who bought this pasuk, please help me right away."

The host looked perplexed, not understanding why this was a major emergency, and Reb Dovid clarified it for him.

"Look, whoever bought this pasuk is obviously either unwell, or has a close relative or friend who is unwell. They are likely buying it as a zechus for someone who is sick, and I need to know the name of that person so that I can daven for them! How can I wait another moment?"

בָּרוּךְ אַתָּה יהוה אֱלֹהֵינוּ מֶלֶךְ הָעוֹלָם,
אֲשֶׁר קִדְּשָׁנוּ בְּמִצְוֹתָיו, וְצִוָּנוּ עַל
מִצְוַת צִיצִת.

Just as someone who has an oxygen tank and knows of a patient struggling to breathe will hurry, Reb Dovid saw the power of *tefillah* for the awesome force it is, and he could not wait to start davening for a fellow Jew.

It is this bond between Jews that we wish to reinforce at the start of the *tefillah*.

עַל מִצְוַת צִיצִת —
Regarding the commandment of tzitzis.

Even before Reb Zalman was diagnosed with Covid-19, he had little will to go on. The passing of his wife left him lonely and dejected, and when the virus struck him a few weeks later, it sapped him of whatever energy he had left.

His children looked on in alarm as their 90-year-old father, a respected talmid chacham and Rosh Yeshivah, simply gave up, unwilling to cooperate with doctors, uninterested in being moved to the hospital, and generally making it clear that he had little interest in life itself.

It didn't make sense that a man who had learned and davened with such passion and enthusiasm for so long would just give up the chance to serve Hashem in this world, and his children understood that he was suffering from depression.

He said it clearly. He no longer had the head to learn, was too weak to leave his bed, and wasn't sure that his body was clean enough to put on tefillin.

ઍ Putting On Tzitzis ઍ

Blessed are You, HASHEM, our God, King of
the universe, Who has sanctified us with
His commandments, and has commanded us
regarding the commandment of tzitzis.

> Why should he fight?
>
> One of his sons, a close talmid of Rav Dovid
> Soloveitchik, discussed the situation with Rav Dovid.
>
> "Ich farshtei nisht, I don't understand," the Brisker
> Rosh Yeshivah remarked. "Tzitzis trugt ehr? Does he
> wear tzitzis?"
>
> Yes, the son confirmed, his father lay in his bed
> wearing tzitzis.
>
> "So how can he say his life has no meaning if at every
> moment he's fulfilling a mitzvah with immeasurable
> value?"
>
> The son repeated Rav Dovid's words to his father,
> who contemplated them for a long moment. The effect
> was more profound than any medication or treatment;
> the patient sat up straight, color returning to his face as
> he pondered this thought.
>
> He was wearing tzitzis!

At every moment, he was encircled by a mitzvah, connecting him to Hashem and fulfilling the purpose of existence. This
thought restored his will to go on, and within a few weeks, he
was feeling better, able to return to yeshivah once again and
say *shiur*.

> The great Vilna Gaon was crying on his deathbed,
> and his students asked him, "Why are you crying?"
> He held up his tzitzis fringes and said, "In this world,
> for just a few kopecks we can buy a few strings and
> do a mitzvah at every moment. In the Next World, it is
> impossible to do a mitzvah."

⧽ עֲטִיפַת טַלִּית ⧼

For complete procedure turn to page 130.

בָּרוּךְ אַתָּה יהוה אֱלֹהֵינוּ מֶלֶךְ הָעוֹלָם, אֲשֶׁר קִדְּשָׁנוּ בְּמִצְוֹתָיו, וְצִוָּנוּ לְהִתְעַטֵּף בַּצִּיצִת.

⧽ הֲנָחַת תְּפִילִין ⧼

For complete procedure turn to page 134.

תְּפִלִין שֶׁל יָד

בָּרוּךְ אַתָּה יהוה אֱלֹהֵינוּ מֶלֶךְ הָעוֹלָם, אֲשֶׁר קִדְּשָׁנוּ בְּמִצְוֹתָיו, וְצִוָּנוּ לְהָנִיחַ תְּפִלִּין.

תְּפִלִין שֶׁל רֹאשׁ

בָּרוּךְ אַתָּה יהוה אֱלֹהֵינוּ מֶלֶךְ הָעוֹלָם, אֲשֶׁר קִדְּשָׁנוּ בְּמִצְוֹתָיו, וְצִוָּנוּ עַל מִצְוַת תְּפִלִּין.

Tzitzis symbolizes the rich spiritual opportunities in this world, and this idea fills us with enthusiasm and joy.

Perhaps this is one of the reasons we kiss the *tzitzis*, a sign of love and appreciation for a mitzvah that is constantly within reach, encircling us and allowing us constant connection to the Creator. The Torah gives us a reason for this mitzvah: לְמַעַן תִּזְכְּרוּ, *So that you may remember* (*Bamidbar* 15:40). Beholding these strings reminds a person that we were created for a reason, and remembering the mission with which we were charged brings us a bit closer to that goal.

Now, as we have contemplated the blessings with which we are surrounded, aware of His presence and His kindness in returning our souls and allowing us another day in His world, we are inspired to lead lives free of sin, reveling in His holy embrace.

✎ Putting On the Tallis ✎

For complete procedure turn to page 130.

*B*lessed are You, HASHEM, our God, King of the universe, Who has sanctified us with His commandments and has commanded us to wrap ourselves in tzitzis.

✎ Putting On Tefillin ✎

For complete procedure turn to page 134.

ARM TEFILLIN

*B*lessed are You, HASHEM, our God, King of the universe, Who has sanctified us with His commandments and has commanded us to put on tefillin.

HEAD TEFILLIN

*B*lessed are You, Hashem, our God, King of the universe, Who has sanctified us with His commandments and has commanded us regarding the commandment of tefillin.

לְהָנִיחַ תְּפִלִּין —
To put on tefillin.

The young man who sat before the Chazon Ish was quite honest: he simply experienced no joy, no pride, no feeling at all in doing mitzvos. It was just an action, with no emotional reaction, he said.

The Chazon Ish was quiet for a moment, and then addressed his visitor. "Know this, my son," he said. "It is worth it for the *neshamah* to make the lengthy trip to this world and to experience suffering for eighty years… if only to don *tefillin* just once!"

מַה טֹּבוּ אֹהָלֶיךָ יַעֲקֹב, מִשְׁכְּנֹתֶיךָ יִשְׂרָאֵל. וַאֲנִי

Rav Itzikel of Pshevorsk would recall the day he first put on *tefillin*. His father had taken him to Shineve, where the Divrei Yechezkel wrapped *tefillin* around the arms of the young boy for the first time.

"When you wrap the *tefillin* around your arms seven times," the Shinever Rebbe said, "don't merely count to seven, but rather, contemplate the seven words in the pasuk: וְאַתֶּם הַדְּבֵקִים בַּה' אֱלֹהֵיכֶם חַיִּים כֻּלְּכֶם הַיּוֹם, *But you who cleave to the Lord, your God, are alive, all of you, this day* (*Devarim* 4:4).

"From that day," the Pshevorsker Rebbe remarked, "I have never forgotten the *kavannah* taught to me by the Shinever Rebbe."

Tefillin connect us to the Source of Life, its straps binding us to eternity and connecting us with the Creator.

The straps are wrapped around the finger as well, symbolizing a ring with which we are wed to the Ribbono Shel Olam. Therefore, as we wrap the *tefillin* around our middle finger, we say the *pasuk*, וְאֵרַשְׂתִּיךְ לִי לְעוֹלָם, *And I will betroth you to Me forever* (*Hoshea* 2:21).

The Chofetz Chaim observed the struggles of the poverty-stricken yeshivos in Europe, the diligent, committed *bachurim* facing intense hunger, day after day. He called together an *asifah* of Rabbanim and philanthropists, hoping to find a solution. The Chofetz Chaim's deep pain was evident, and that night, Rav Shmuel Greineman found himself unable to sleep. The image of the pained *gadol hador* allowed him no rest, and he contemplated the issue throughout the night.

By morning, he had an idea, which he presented to the Chofetz Chaim.

It is well known, he said, that the reward for putting on *tefillin* one time is worth the entire world. Rav Shmuel offered to donate his *schar*, the reward for putting on *tefillin* once, and

How goodly are your tents, O Yaakov, your dwelling places, O Yisrael.[1] As for me,

(1) *Bamidbar* 24:5.

in that merit, the Ribbono Shel Olam would sustain all of the *bnei yeshivah* in Europe.

The Chofetz Chaim heard the idea and responded with a *mashal* of a little boy who finds money lying on a street corner, bills worth thousands of rubles. The excited child grabs the folded bills and runs to the candy store, hoping to trade them for a candy. If the owner of the store is an honest man, he will never accept the money. He will tell the child that the bills are worth much more than the candy, and the boy must bring the money back home to his father.

The Chofetz Chaim explained to Rav Shmuel that putting on *tefillin* even one time is worth so much more than feeding all of the *bnei yeshivah* in Europe. "The Ribbono Shel Olam," the Chofetz Chaim concluded, "will never be able to accept the deal."

For simply donning *tefillin*, just once, the reward is greater than anything this world has to offer.

מַה טֹּבוּ אֹהָלֶיךָ יַעֲקֹב, מִשְׁכְּנֹתֶיךָ יִשְׂרָאֵל —
How goodly are your tents, O Yaakov,
your dwelling places, O Yisrael.

These words recited by Bilaam HaRasha lead us into the *beis haknesses*, a proclamation of gratitude and pride in our "dwelling places." What are the dwelling places referred to here? The Gemara (*Sanhedrin* 105b) relates that this was an attempt by Bilaam to curse us, which was transformed into blessing. He wanted to curse our nation that we should not have *batei knessios* and *batei midrashos*, but he was forced to bless us instead.

Rashi, however (*Bamidbar* 24:5), says that Bilaam was

praising Klal Yisrael over the fact that the entrances to their tents were not facing each other, thereby ensuring their modesty and privacy. Rashi sees the tents and dwellings of the *pasuk* as a reference to Jewish homes.

It would seem that there is a message here about what makes Klal Yisrael unique, and it was this aspect that Bilaam was admiring. Unlike in other beliefs, where the house of prayer is sacred and the home mundane, our homes are likewise saturated with *kedushah*, the spirit of the shul extending there as well, with modesty, kindness, and respect alive and well between their walls.

> *Reb Berel Ludmir, a distinguished Boyaner chassid, was ailing and not able to leave his home. The Beis Yisrael of Ger came to visit Reb Berel, with whom he had a close relationship. Reb Berel, who had been a frequent participant in the Gerrer Rebbe's tisch, shared his pain. "Ich benk zich, I miss taking part in the Rebbe's tisch," he told the Rebbe.*
>
> *The Gerrer Rebbe asked Reb Berel where he learned Torah, and Reb Berel indicated the adjacent table. The Rebbe reached out and tapped the table. He quoted a pasuk,* זֶה הַשֻּׁלְחָן אֲשֶׁר לִפְנֵי ה', *"This is the table that is before Hashem" (Yechezkel 41:22), as he looked at Reb Berel. "This is a tisch," he said. "This is a tisch."*
>
> *With a few words, the Rebbe had invested the avodah, the Torah and tefillah of a homebound chassid, with the glory of a crowded chassidic beis medrash, enabling him to feel part of the reflected light in his own home.*
>
> *When we live elevated lives, our dwellings can also carry within them the radiance of the shul.*
>
> *And perhaps there is another message here as well, underscoring what it means to join with other Jews to form a minyan in shul.*
>
> *There was a Jew who davened Shacharis at the Kosel each morning, joining a vasikin minyan that included Rav Moshe Shapira.*

The wife of this Jew was diagnosed with a medical condition, and the couple consulted with two different doctors. Both professionals had different approaches to treating the illness, and each was confident that only his method was effective.

The woman, the patient herself, very much wanted to consult with a great talmid chacham. Her husband, who davened with Rav Moshe Shapira each morning and saw the intensity of his tefillos, wanted to ask Rav Moshe for advice.

They didn't have any sort of personal connection, however, and when the gentleman called the Rav's assistant to schedule an appointment, he was told that the next available time slot was months away.

A few days later, after Shacharis, the Jew approached Rav Moshe to say good morning. Rav Moshe returned the greeting, and the concerned husband shared his pain, telling Rav Moshe about his difficulty in obtaining an appointment with the Rav within a realistic time frame. Rav Moshe listened, but said little.

The next morning, Rav Moshe approached this man after Shacharis and asked if they might go to his house and speak with his wife. Together, they walked through the Old City, to the man's apartment.

Inside, Rav Moshe listened, counseled, discussed, advised, and warmly blessed. He spent over an hour with this couple.

As the Rav prepared to leave, the host innocently asked, "Harav, can I ask what is going on? Does the Rav have time or does he not have time? If the Rav doesn't have time, then how did he spend an hour with us this morning? If the Rav does have time, then why was I given an appointment that was months away?"

Rav Moshe Shapira looked at him with a serious expression. "In truth, I do not have time. But if it was a family emergency, I would do whatever I could, whether or not I had time. And Yidden who daven

בְּרֹב חַסְדְּךָ אָבוֹא בֵיתֶךָ, אֶשְׁתַּחֲוֶה אֶל הֵיכַל קָדְשְׁךָ בְּיִרְאָתֶךָ. ² יְהוָה אָהַבְתִּי מְעוֹן בֵּיתֶךָ, וּמְקוֹם מִשְׁכַּן כְּבוֹדֶךָ. ³ וַאֲנִי אֶשְׁתַּחֲוֶה וְאֶכְרָעָה, אֶבְרְכָה לִפְנֵי יְהוָה עֹשִׂי. ⁴ וַאֲנִי, תְפִלָּתִי לְךָ יְהוָה עֵת רָצוֹן, אֱלֹהִים בְּרָב חַסְדֶּךָ, עֲנֵנִי בֶּאֱמֶת יִשְׁעֶךָ. ⁵

together each morning," Rav Moshe concluded, "they are also a family."

This is the element of home within the shul. People who join in creating a *minyan* are a unit, bonded together as a single force.

Our homes have the light of our shuls, and our shuls reflect the relationship that exists within our homes.

Mah tovu ohalecha…

❦

The Gemara (*Sanhedrin* 105b) tells us that even though Bilaam was compelled to replace the curses with blessings, all the curses he had conceived of in his heart ended up befalling Klal Yisrael, except for one of them — "*Ohalecha Yaakov,* your tents, O Yaakov."

It might be, says Rav Yitzchok Sorotzkin, that these tents are so essential to our existence as a nation, so imperative to our very essence, that they cannot be taken away, for Klal Yisrael must endure. The world exists only for us, and these *batei knessios* are the foundation upon which we rest — and so these holy tents remain, despite his plan to curse them.

This is another reason why we begin the day with the words of this *rasha*, Bilaam. Here we see just how precious our shuls are, how necessary our *tefillah b'tzibbur* is, and with this in mind, we can start to pray.

through Your abundant kindness I will enter Your House; I will prostrate myself toward Your Holy Sanctuary in awe of You.[2] *O HASHEM, I love the House where You dwell, and the place where Your glory resides.*[3] *I shall prostrate myself and bow, I shall kneel before HASHEM my Maker.*[4] *As for me, may my prayer to You, HASHEM, be at a favorable time; O God, in Your abundant kindness, answer me with the truth of Your salvation.*[5]

(2) *Tehillim* 5:8. (3) 26:8. (4) Cf. 95:6. (5) 69:14.

וַאֲנִי בְּרֹב חַסְדְּךָ אָבוֹא בֵיתֶךָ,
אֶשְׁתַּחֲוֶה אֶל הֵיכַל קָדְשְׁךָ בְּיִרְאָתֶךָ —

As for me, through Your abundant kindness I will enter Your House; I will prostrate myself toward Your Holy Sanctuary in awe of You (Tehillim 5:8).

In generations past, this *pasuk* was used to count whether there were enough men present to form a *minyan* since it contains ten words, a fitting introduction to prayer.

Rav Mattisyahu Salomon once delivered a *shmuess* about the way people casually say, "I am running to Minchah," or "I'll daven in that *beis medrash* today." The assumption is that one will leave his home and easily reach the shul; a person rarely stops to contemplate the miracle of simply going from one place to another safely, and all the hurdles that might have arisen along the way.

And so, before we start to daven, to express reverence and gratitude, we begin with a simple thanks. We are grateful for the fact that we have reached shul. It is only *b'rov chasdecha*, through Your abundant kindness, that *avo veisecha*, we are able to enter Your house.

אֲדוֹן עוֹלָם אֲשֶׁר מָלַךְ בְּטֶרֶם כָּל יְצִיר נִבְרָא.
לְעֵת נַעֲשָׂה בְחֶפְצוֹ כֹּל, אֲזַי מֶלֶךְ
שְׁמוֹ נִקְרָא. וְאַחֲרֵי כִּכְלוֹת הַכֹּל, לְבַדּוֹ יִמְלוֹךְ
נוֹרָא. וְהוּא הָיָה וְהוּא הֹוֶה, וְהוּא יִהְיֶה בְּתִפְאָרָה.
וְהוּא אֶחָד וְאֵין שֵׁנִי לְהַמְשִׁיל לוֹ לְהַחְבִּירָה.

אֲדוֹן עוֹלָם אֲשֶׁר מָלַךְ בְּטֶרֶם כָּל יְצִיר נִבְרָא —
*Master of the universe, Who reigned before
any form was created.*

This *tefillah,* authored by *Kadmonim* (some attribute it to
Rav Sherira Gaon, others to R' Shlomo Ibn Gabirol), has the
power to "cut through the *mekatregim,*" the forces that would
attempt to block our *tefillos* from rising. "I do not know of
any *chachamim,*" writes Rav Chaim Palagi, "who would miss
reciting this *tefillah.*"

The *Mateh Moshe* brings a "*segulah,*" a way to merit a good
judgment on Rosh Hashanah and Yom Kippur. He quotes R'
Yehudah HaChassid, Rav Hai Gaon, and Rav Sherira Gaon,
who say that "One who concentrates when reciting *Adon
Olam* is guaranteed that his *tefillah* is heard. No Satan can
block it, and there will be no obstacle or evil mishap on Rosh
Hashanah and Yom Kippur."[1]

When the *Malach* Michael hears this *tefillah,* writes Rav
Yaakov Rekach, he brings it before Hashem.

Rav Pinchas of Polotzk authored a commentary on the siddur that he titled *Maggid Tzedek.* He brought it to the Vilna
Gaon for a *haskamah.* The Gaon opened it and read just one
thought, but he was so impressed by it that he immediately
gave his approbation, saying that the entire commentary was
worth it if only for this single explanation.

---

1. For this reason, many congregations recite this *piyut* together on the morning
   of Rosh Hashanah and Yom Kippur, using a traditional tune.

*Master of the universe, Who reigned before any
form was created. At the time when His will
brought all into being — then as "King" was
His Name proclaimed. After all has ceased to be,
He, the Awesome One, will reign alone. It is He
Who was, He Who is, and He Who shall remain,
in splendor. He is One — there is no second
to compare to Him, to declare as His equal.*

What was the insight that so impressed the Gra? Rav
Pinchas suggested that we begin *tefillas* Shacharis with the
tefillah of *Adon Olam* because Shacharis was instituted by
Avraham Avinu, who was the first to call Hashem *Adon,*
Master (*Berachos* 7b).

(Rav Berel Soloveitchik of Brisk asked his father, the Brisker
Rav, why the Gaon had been so enthusiastic about an insight
that would seem to be relatively simple.

"Because the Gaon was an *ish emes,*" the Rav replied, "a
man of truth, and the *pshat* is *emes*; and *emes* is *emes, nisht
duh aza zach vi a kleine emes udder a groisse emes,* there is no
such thing as a small truth or big truth!")

וְהוּא אֶחָד וְאֵין שֵׁנִי —
He is One — there is no second.

Sometimes, a person's advantage regarding another can
be seen only by comparison: both are big, but one is bigger.
The fact that the comparison with the second one must be
used to describe the first is a limitation in the greatness of the
first one.

With regard to the Ribbono Shel Olam, He is not greater
by comparison to anything else, but by His very essence. He
is "*echad,*" One, the Source of everything, and there is no
"*sheni,*" no second, no comparable force against which He is
measured.

בְּלִי רֵאשִׁית בְּלִי תַכְלִית, וְלוֹ הָעֹז וְהַמִּשְׂרָה.
וְהוּא אֵלִי וְחַי גּוֹאֲלִי, וְצוּר חֶבְלִי בְּעֵת צָרָה.
וְהוּא נִסִּי וּמָנוֹס לִי, מְנָת כּוֹסִי בְּיוֹם אֶקְרָא.

וְהוּא אֵלִי וְחַי גּוֹאֲלִי —
He is my God, my living Redeemer.

Rav Shimon Sofer, son of the Chasam Sofer and Rav in Krakow, once met Rav Shlomo Zalman Breuer, son-in-law of Rav Samson Raphael Hirsch and Rav Hirsch's successor as Rav of Frankfurt.

Rav Shimon asked Rav Breuer to relate a *dvar Torah* from Rav Hirsch, and Rav Breuer shared the following thought.

In *Adon Olam*, we say וְהוּא אֵלִי, *He is my God*. Rav Hirsch taught that after we praise Hakadosh Baruch Hu as the Master of the entire universe, Ruler over all of creation, we continue by saying that He is also "**my** God." Hashem has a personal, real, vibrant connection with every single human being within creation as well.

That is what is meant by וְהוּא אֵלִי against the backdrop of the fact that He is the *Adon Olam*: Yes, Hashem controls every single detail in the universe, but He is the personal God of every person within it as well. This is the introduction to *tefillah*, the reminder that wherever a person is, and however he views himself, Hashem is "his" God, waiting to hear his *tefillos*.

Having a personal God, a Creator attuned to and waiting for the *tefillos* of the individual, is the greatest testimony to what a Yid is and what he is capable of. We open our *tefillos* with this thought because it provides the means to realize the power of our prayers.

In the words of Rav Nochum of Chernobyl, in the *Likkutim*: "Something that has no beginning also has no end, and every single Jew carries within him a spark of Hakadosh Baruch Hu. Therefore, since Hashem is without limit, with no start or

Without beginning, without conclusion —
His is the power and dominion. He is my
God, my living Redeemer, Rock of my pain in
time of distress. He is my banner, a refuge for
me, the portion in my cup on the day I call.

finish, so too every single individual within Klal Yisrael is now
without limit."

וְחַי גּוֹאֲלִי — *My living Redeemer.*

Rav Hirsch explains that a *goel*, redeemer, doesn't just help;
a *goel* is the one who comes to the fore to save a person from
ruin. Hakadosh Baruch Hu is referred to as a *Goel* in Mitzrayim
against the backdrop of describing the suffering of the Bnei
Yisrael. *I am the Lord, and I will take you out from under the*
burdens of Egypt, and I will save you from their labor, and
I will redeem you with an outstretched arm and with great
judgments (*Shemos* 6:6).

Similarly, the *goel* is described by the *pasuk* in regard to a
landowner in distress. The *pasuk* first tells us about the distress of the seller. *If your brother becomes destitute and sells*
some of his inherited property, his redeemer who is related to
him shall come forth and redeem his brother's sale (*Vayikra*
25:25).

Referring to Hakadosh Baruch Hu as a *goel* is acknowledging a Divine *middah* according to which, even if a person
doesn't merit mercy and benevolence, still, the very fact that
he is in trouble makes him eligible for salvation, for Hashem
is the ultimate *Goel*.

וְהוּא נִסִּי וּמָנוֹס לִי, מְנָת כּוֹסִי בְּיוֹם אֶקְרָא —
He is my banner, a refuge for me,
the portion in my cup on the day I call.

Rav Shimon Schwab explains that in times of war, when a

בְּיָדוֹ אַפְקִיד רוּחִי בְּעֵת אִישַׁן וְאָעִירָה. וְעִם רוּחִי גְּוִיָּתִי, יהוה לִי וְלֹא אִירָא.

יִגְדַּל אֱלֹהִים חַי וְיִשְׁתַּבַּח, נִמְצָא וְאֵין עֵת אֶל מְצִיאוּתוֹ. אֶחָד וְאֵין יָחִיד כְּיִחוּדוֹ, נֶעְלָם וְגַם אֵין סוֹף לְאַחְדוּתוֹ. אֵין לוֹ דְּמוּת הַגּוּף וְאֵינוֹ גוּף, לֹא נַעֲרוֹךְ אֵלָיו קְדֻשָּׁתוֹ. קַדְמוֹן לְכָל דָּבָר אֲשֶׁר נִבְרָא, רִאשׁוֹן וְאֵין רֵאשִׁית

soldier is faltering and feels like he has no will to go on, he will raise his eyes to the banner waving high above, the flag to which he pledges allegiance, and he will access renewed energy.

A Yid endures the long, dark *galus*, but every so often he needs *chizuk*, a new source of strength. For that, he looks to his banner, the secret of that strength — the fact that we are Hashem's chosen nation, and His Name rests upon us and within us.

ה' לִי וְלֹא אִירָא —
Hashem is with me, I shall not fear.

Rav Shimshon Pincus would quote the words of the *pasuk*, יוֹם אִירָא אֲנִי אֵלֶיךָ אֶבְטָח, *The day I fear, I will hope to you* (*Tehillim* 56:4). Before one has true *bitachon*, he first has to realize the magnitude of his troubles: only then can he be regarded as having real faith in Hashem's salvation. Hence, יוֹם אִירָא, one should first contemplate how frightening the situation is, and then — like a child jumping joyfully into a swimming pool on a hot summer day — אֲנִי אֵלֶיךָ אֶבְטָח, man can leap into a well-spring of faith, confident and tranquil.

True trust is only when one is not oblivious to potential

Into His hand I shall entrust my spirit when I go to sleep — and I shall awaken! With my spirit shall my body remain. HASHEM is with me, I shall not fear.

Exalted be the Living God and praised, He exists — unbounded by time is His existence. He is One — and there is no unity like His Oneness. Inscrutable and infinite is His Oneness. He has no semblance of a body nor has He a body; and nothing compares to His holiness. He preceded every being that was created — the First, and nothing precedes

---

danger, but perfectly aware; and even with that awareness, he is calm and tranquil, reliant only on the Master of the universe.

יִגְדַּל אֱלֹהִים חַי וְיִשְׁתַּבַּח —
Exalted be the Living God and praised.

This *tefillah,* authored by *Kadmonim,* is a synopsis of the Thirteen *Ikkarim,* the Rambam's principles of faith that many people recite after the morning *tefillah.*

The opening words, *the Living God,* refer to the first principle, *Metzius,* the existence of Hashem.

Then comes *He is One,* referring to the second principle, that of His Oneness.

The words *He has no semblance of a body* correspond to the third principle, "He is not physical."

He preceded every being that was created, as the fourth principle states, means that He is "the very first and He is the very last." Hashem had no beginning and He has no end. He is infinite.

He is the Master of the universe, reflecting the fifth principle, "To Him alone it is proper to pray," and then we express

לְרֵאשִׁיתוֹ. הִנּוֹ אֲדוֹן עוֹלָם לְכָל נוֹצָר, יוֹרֶה
גְדֻלָּתוֹ וּמַלְכוּתוֹ. שֶׁפַע נְבוּאָתוֹ נְתָנוֹ, אֶל אַנְשֵׁי
סְגֻלָּתוֹ וְתִפְאַרְתּוֹ. לֹא קָם בְּיִשְׂרָאֵל כְּמֹשֶׁה עוֹד,
נָבִיא וּמַבִּיט אֶת תְּמוּנָתוֹ. תּוֹרַת אֱמֶת נָתַן לְעַמּוֹ
אֵל, עַל יַד נְבִיאוֹ נֶאֱמַן בֵּיתוֹ. לֹא יַחֲלִיף הָאֵל
וְלֹא יָמִיר דָּתוֹ, לְעוֹלָמִים לְזוּלָתוֹ. צוֹפֶה וְיוֹדֵעַ
סְתָרֵינוּ, מַבִּיט לְסוֹף דָּבָר בְּקַדְמָתוֹ. גּוֹמֵל לְאִישׁ
חֶסֶד כְּמִפְעָלוֹ, נוֹתֵן לְרָשָׁע רָע כְּרִשְׁעָתוֹ. יִשְׁלַח
לְקֵץ הַיָּמִין מְשִׁיחֵנוּ, לִפְדּוֹת מְחַכֵּי קֵץ יְשׁוּעָתוֹ.

the fact that *He granted His flow of prophecy to His treasured splendrous people,* which is the sixth principle, that of
Divine prophecy through *Neviim*. *In Israel none like Moshe
arose again* reflects the seventh principle, that "Moshe was
the patriarch of the prophets."

God gave His people a Torah of truth corresponds to the
eighth principle, that "the Torah that is found in our hands is
the same one given to Moshe, our teacher." *God will never
amend nor exchange the Torah,* as we say in the ninth principle, "this Torah will not be exchanged."

He scrutinizes and knows our hiddenmost secrets, as
the tenth principle states, "That the Creator, blessed is His
Name, knows all the deeds of human beings and all their
thoughts."

*He recompenses man with kindness according to his
deed; He assigns evil to the wicked according to his
wickedness* tells us the truth of Divine reward and punishment, as the eleventh principle states, "That the Creator,
blessed is His Name, rewards with good those who observe
His commandments and punishes those who violate His
commandments."

His precedence. Behold! He is Master of the universe to every creature; He demonstrates His greatness and His sovereignty. He granted His flow of prophecy to His treasured, splendrous people. In Israel none like Moshe arose again — a prophet who perceived His vision clearly. God gave His people a Torah of truth, by means of His prophet, the most trusted of His household. God will never amend nor exchange His law for any other one, for all eternity. He scrutinizes and knows our hiddenmost secrets; He perceives a matter's outcome from its start. He recompenses man with kindness according to his deed; He assigns evil to the wicked according to his wickedness. By the End of Days He will send our Mashiach, to redeem those longing for His final salvation.

By the End of Days He will send our Mashiach to redeem us proclaims the truth of the twelfth principle, "I believe with complete faith in the coming of Mashiach."

And finally, we conclude with our confidence that *God will revive the dead in His abundant kindness,* the thirteenth principle of *Techiyas HaMeisim,* "whenever there arises the will for it from the Creator, blessed is His Name."

— גּוֹמֵל לְאִישׁ חֶסֶד כְּמִפְעָלוֹ, נוֹתֵן לְרָשָׁע רָע כְּרִשְׁעָתוֹ
He recompenses man with kindness according to his deed; He assigns evil to the wicked according to his wickedness.

Why does the language change from גּוֹמֵל, *recompenses,* to נוֹתֵן, *assigns?* Additionally, why is kindness repaid according to the "deed," and wickedness only in proportion to the

מֵתִים יְחַיֶּה אֵל בְּרֹב חַסְדּוֹ, בָּרוּךְ עֲדֵי עַד שֵׁם
תְּהִלָּתוֹ.

בָּרוּךְ אַתָּה יהוה אֱלֹהֵינוּ מֶלֶךְ הָעוֹלָם, אֲשֶׁר
קִדְּשָׁנוּ בְּמִצְוֹתָיו, וְצִוָּנוּ עַל נְטִילַת יָדָיִם.

בָּרוּךְ אַתָּה יהוה אֱלֹהֵינוּ מֶלֶךְ הָעוֹלָם, אֲשֶׁר
יָצַר אֶת הָאָדָם בְּחָכְמָה, וּבָרָא בּוֹ

wickedness? Why not use the same word — כְּמִפְעָלוֹ, *according to his deed* —for both, or utilize a consistent theme and say that the man of kindness is repaid "according to his righteousness"?

The holy Rebbe of Ruzhin explained this with the example of a man so poor that he cannot afford to buy even a pair of shoes. A generous person notices this and buys a pair of new shoes, which he presents to the pauper.

The effects of the gift are immediately apparent. The recipient can now walk with dignity, able to go where he wishes to in his comfortable shoes, and he has a new sense of self-respect as well. The shoes might well be the reason he can look for a job and perhaps find gainful employment, no longer reduced to begging. A cycle is started, all because of the shoes, and, says the Ruzhiner, Hakadosh Baruch Hu is גּוֹמֵל, He generously dispenses rewards not merely for the gift of the shoes themselves, but כְּמִפְעָלוֹ, according to what the act has spawned. All the good that follows is also credited to the original donor, who simply gave a pair of shoes.

But regarding wickedness, the opposite is true. If someone cruelly takes the shoes of another, leaving him without the means to walk comfortably, the punishment is only for the act itself, not for what it causes.

This is a kindness of Hashem, the One Who is trusted to reward and punish.

God will revive the dead in His abundant kindness — Blessed forever is His praised Name.

Blessed are You, HASHEM, our God, King of the universe, Who has sanctified us with His commandments and has commanded us regarding washing the hands

Blessed are You, HASHEM, our God, King of the universe, Who fashioned man with wisdom and created within him many

וְצִוָּנוּ עַל נְטִילַת יָדָיִם —
And has commanded us regarding washing the hands.

The word used here is not *rechitzah*, which means "washing," but *netilah*, which means "receiving." This is because the act of washing hands at the start of the day is not merely performed for cleanliness and purity, but in order to elevate our hands. We are taking them from one place to another, marking them not just as agents of mundane activity, but as the means through which we can create eternity.

אֲשֶׁר יָצַר אֶת הָאָדָם בְּחָכְמָה —
Who fashioned man with wisdom.

This *berachah* is recited before *tefillah* so that a person can approach prayer with a clean body, ready for an encounter with the King. This *berachah* is so central to the start of a new day that some *poskim* rule that even if a person doesn't attend to his bodily functions, he should nevertheless recite this *berachah* upon awakening.

This *berachah* begins with a reference to *chochmah*. There

נְקָבִים נְקָבִים, חֲלוּלִים חֲלוּלִים. גָּלוּי
וְיָדוּעַ לִפְנֵי כִסֵּא כְבוֹדֶךָ, שֶׁאִם יִפָּתֵחַ אֶחָד
מֵהֶם, אוֹ יִסָּתֵם אֶחָד מֵהֶם, אִי אֶפְשָׁר
לְהִתְקַיֵּם וְלַעֲמוֹד לְפָנֶיךָ (אֲפִילוּ שָׁעָה אֶחָת).

are conflicting opinions as to whether this refers to the wisdom involved in the creation of man or the wisdom with which
man was imbued. It concludes by discussing a *pele*, wonder
— וּמַפְלִיא לַעֲשׂוֹת. The precision, meticulousness, and incredi-
ble wisdom that is evident in the human being is itself a wonder, worthy of contemplation and awe.

Rav Yechezkel Levenstein would recite this *berachah* with
tremendous concentration and feeling. "Is this any less of a
miracle than that of the splitting of the *Yam Suf*?" he asked his
talmidim. "Even the most well-crafted machine needs repairs
to keep it running smoothly, yet this extraordinarily elaborate
creation — man — functions smoothly, with no blockages or
breakdowns. It is nothing less than an open *neis*, and contemplation of that wonder is itself a *segulah* to remain healthy."

Rav Nota Freund, one of the *tzaddikim* of the Holy City and
a legendary *melamed* in the Etz Chaim *cheder*, would repeat
that which he received from Rav Shlom'ke of Zhvil.

There are five basic *kavannos*, areas of focus, to have in
mind when reciting this *berachah*, taught the *tzaddik* of Zhvil.

— Imagine the gratitude a person feels after successfully
surviving major surgery, which might have resulted in
his death.

— A surgery that was performed by the most respected
and sought-after doctor in the country.

— Which, intricate and complex as it is, still requires no
anesthetic, allowing the patient to remain awake.

— A procedure that involves the entire body yet comes with
no side effects and leaves no pain.

openings and many cavities. It is obvious and known before Your Throne of Glory that if but one of them were to be ruptured or but one of them were to be blocked, it would be impossible to survive and to stand before You (for even one hour).

— A life-saving operation, performed free of charge, at no expense to the patient.

This happens every single time a person relieves himself, the Rebbe taught; each of these five miracles is a reason for intense thanksgiving.

A chassid overheard his Rebbe, the Beis Aharon of Karlin, reciting *Asher Yatzar* to the tune generally used for *Hallel*, and the chassid smiled. The Rebbe turned to him. "Is this *berachah* and what it represents not significant enough to merit the same concentration and gratitude as the *Hallel* we say each month?"

נְקָבִים נְקָבִים, חֲלוּלִים חֲלוּלִים —
Many openings and many cavities.

Why are the words "openings" and "cavities" doubled?

This hints at the close of the *berachah*, which refers to the fusion of *neshamah* and *guf,* the spiritual and physical. The body is real, but the essence of man is the soul, and together they create eternity.

The double language refers to this synthesis of two different dimensions within man.

Rav Shimon Schwab explains this with a fascinating insight. If a righteous person requires a heart transplant, and the organ given to him had previously belonged to a wicked person, the recipient will not suddenly become wicked — rather, the opposite will occur. The heart will become a "good heart."

This, says Rav Schwab, is because the physical organ is

just a reflection of the spiritual one; it is the spiritual, intangible, invisible part of the body, not its physical parallel, that defines a person.

According to the *Levush*, the two openings are a reference to the way food enters the body, and also the way that it exits the body. Both are equal *chassadim*: the fact that we receive the nourishment we need, and also that the body rejects those parts of food that don't serve its physical requirements.

גָּלוּי וְיָדוּעַ לִפְנֵי כִסֵּא כְבוֹדֶךָ —
It is obvious and known before
Your Throne of Glory.

The fact that man would be unable to survive, even for a moment, without the smooth functioning of his body is known to all, not just before the Heavenly Throne. Why, then, do we refer only to the fact that it is revealed before the Master of the universe?

At times, a doctor will offer an assessment based on medical knowledge, stating that a medical problem has no solution, or the opposite, deciding that an apparently serious illness is actually trivial. The diagnosis may be wrong, but no one is aware except the Creator: only He truly knows the realities of our medical situations, and this is the tribute we tender in this *berachah*.

We offer thanks and praise to the only One before Whom all the secrets are revealed. Medical knowledge is limited, but His knowledge is unlimited, and if we are able to survive, it is only because of His boundless love and kindness.

גָּלוּי וְיָדוּעַ לִפְנֵי כִסֵּא כְבוֹדֶךָ —
It is obvious and known before
Your Throne of Glory.

The Raavan, quoted in *Siddur HaGra*, explains the reference to the Throne of Glory specifically in this *berachah*. It is to express that nothing, no detail, is too unimportant to the Ribbono Shel Olam. The internal workings of man are also conducted by Heaven, significant and relevant before Him, in His place of glory.

In the words of the Or HaChaim HaKadosh (*Shemos* 22:6): "There is no hour or instant in the day in which Hashem Yisbarach is not performing an action on behalf of a person, seeing to his most basic needs."

שֶׁאִם יִפָּתַח אֶחָד מֵהֶם, אוֹ יִסָּתֵם אֶחָד מֵהֶם,

אִי אֶפְשָׁר לְהִתְקַיֵּם וְלַעֲמֹד לְפָנֶיךָ (אֲפִילוּ שָׁעָה אֶחָת) —

That if but one of them were to be ruptured or but one of them were to be blocked, it would be impossible to survive and to stand before You (even for one hour).

Rav Yechezkel Abramsky once told his *talmidim* about how he had been a sickly, weak child and was often compelled to remain at home due to one illness or another. This continued until, at over forty years of age, he was sentenced to five years of hard labor in Siberia, without the protection of warm clothing.

When the Rav arrived in the freezing Russian tundra, he offered a prayer.

The Ribbono Shel Olam sends the elements, heat and cold, and man is charged with protecting himself appropriately. Rabbi Chanina said, "Everything is in the hands of Heaven except for sickness from cold and heat" (*Bava Basra* 144b).

What this means is that although weather conditions are, of course, ordained by Heaven, a person can take precautions to ensure they don't affect him, such as buying warm clothing, remaining indoors, or being properly nourished.

"But Ribbono Shel Olam," Rav Abramsky said, "here, there is no way to protect myself from the fierce cold, living in a flimsy hut and spending long hours outside. Here, I turn to You to protect me, for I cannot protect myself!"

During the years he spent in Siberia, Rav Abramsky testified that he never even got a cold, his health completely in the hands of the Creator. So sheltered was he that it was during those years, alone, with little food and no *sefarim*,

בָּרוּךְ אַתָּה יהוה, רוֹפֵא כָל בָּשָׂר וּמַפְלִיא לַעֲשׂוֹת.

that Rav Abramsky authored significant parts of his *Chazon Yechezkel*.

רוֹפֵא כָל בָּשָׂר וּמַפְלִיא לַעֲשׂוֹת —
Who heals all flesh and acts wondrously,

The Rema explains that the words refer to the most wondrous association of all, that of the *neshamah*, the soul, a spark of Divine, with the corporal, physical body. It is the marriage between the spiritual and the material, which is the point of life and all of creation.

Only the "*Mafli la'asos,*" One Who is wondrous in His acts, can fuse the two.

The *neshamah* needs the body to host it — but once they are joined, the soul has the capacity to "pull" the body, to lift it to new heights.

One of the most fundamental teachings of Chassidus was that expounded upon by the Baal HaTanya, that "*hamoach shalit al halev,* the mind rules the heart." Once body and soul are joined, the *neshamah* should be in full control.

> A devoted chassid, Rav Moshe Meisels, would testify that it was this teaching that saved his life.
>
> A scholarly man, Reb Moshe was fluent in several languages, and during Napoleon's war on Russia, he served as a translator for the French high command. The Baal HaTanya, Rav Shneur Zalman, felt that it would be better for the Jewish community if the Russians were victorious, and he instructed his chassid to share French military secrets with the Russian intelligence officers.
>
> At one meeting of the French high command, the door was flung open and Napoleon himself strode into the room. The emperor looked around the room and pointed to Reb Moshe.

Blessed are You, HASHEM, Who heals all flesh and acts wondrously.

"Who is this person?" he asked, and hurried over to Reb Moshe. "You are a spy," Napoleon cried out and immediately placed a hand on Reb Moshe's chest, so that he could feel the pounding heart of a traitor who had been exposed.

But Reb Moshe focused on his Rebbe's teaching, and with his mind firmly in control, he instructed his heart to beat as it usually did.

The Rebbe was right. Reb Moshe was able to steady his heartbeat, and he calmly told the emperor that he was just an interpreter, there to help communicate with the various military personnel in their respective languages.

Napoleon apologized and moved on.

This is the wondrous fusion of *neshamah* and *guf,* mind and matter. Alone, the *neshamah* cannot accomplish in the Heavenly realms; it needs the *guf* to host it. Once it rests within the body, however, the *neshamah* can control the body's every action, elevating the *guf* so that it, too, can reach the Heavens.

This is the wonder of wonders, the creation of man.

Rav Aharon Leib Shteinman once visited Switzerland, where he had lived and taught Torah for several years as a young man. One of his talmidim suggested that they go for a walk amid the soaring mountain peaks and enjoy the glory of Hakadosh Baruch Hu's creation.

Rav Steinman had little interest, and even when they walked along the scenic paths, he didn't raise his eyes or look beyond his own four amos, as was his practice. Eventually, the talmid inquired why the Rosh Yeshivah would not look. "What about the opportunity to behold the splendor of His works? What about perceiving that

It is prohibited to study or recite Torah passages before reciting the following blessings. However, these blessings need not be repeated each time one studies at various times of the day. Although many siddurim begin a new paragraph at וְהַעֲרֶב נָא, "Sweeten, please," according to the vast majority of commentators, the first blessing includes the request of וְהַעֲרֶב נָא.

בָּרוּךְ אַתָּה יהוה אֱלֹהֵינוּ מֶלֶךְ הָעוֹלָם, אֲשֶׁר קִדְּשָׁנוּ בְּמִצְוֹתָיו וְצִוָּנוּ לַעֲסוֹק בְּדִבְרֵי תוֹרָה.

'Mah rabbu ma'asecha Hashem? How great are Your works, O Lord?'" (Tehillim 104:24).

Rav Shteinman smiled and pointed to himself. "To see 'mah rabbu' I don't have to look up at the Alps. It is enough to study my own body and see the wonders and miracles He performs within me, at each and every moment."

One has only to look inward to see the splendor.

Rav Moshe Shapira was once told about a leading secular scientist, an avowed atheist, who revised his opinion late in life. After conducting various experiments and discovering inconceivable wonders within creation, the scholar had reached the scientific conclusion that God exists, and he had written a book celebrating his newfound belief.

Rav Moshe was unimpressed. "*Uch uhn vei,* how piteous it is that a god can be discovered only in a laboratory," he said.

Blessings of the Torah — ברכות התורה

Birchos HaTorah is a *mitzvah d'Oraisa.* We derive this mitzvah from a *pasuk,* according to the Gemara (*Berachos* 21a): "And from where in the Torah do we derive the obligation to recite a blessing prior to studying the Torah? As it is stated: *When I proclaim the Lord's Name, give glory to our God*" (*Devarim* 32:3).

Rav Shneur Zalman of Liadi, in *Shulchan Aruch HaRav* (47:1), elaborates on this Gemara, teaching that a person has

It is prohibited to study or recite Torah passages before reciting the following blessings. However, these blessings need not be repeated each time one studies at various times of the day. Although many siddurim begin a new paragraph at וְהַעֲרֶב נָא, "Sweeten, please," according to the vast majority of commentators, the first blessing includes the request of וְהַעֲרֶב נָא.

Blessed are You, HASHEM, our God, King of the universe, Who has sanctified us with His commandments and has commanded us to engross ourselves in the words of Torah.

to be especially vigilant with regard to reciting the *berachos* over *limud haTorah*, quoting the Gemara (*Nedarim* 81a): "The Land (Eretz Yisrael) was laid to waste only because the people of the time did not recite the blessings that precede Torah study."

Explains the Baal HaTanya: They did not consider the Torah worthy of reciting a blessing prior to learning from it, and therefore, even though they immersed themselves in the words of Torah, it did not protect them. The Torah, Hashem's precious vessel in which He delights every day, should be valued so highly that a person should recite the *berachos* with a joy that surpasses his joy over all the pleasures in the world.

This joy indicates an appreciation and reverence for the Torah itself, and the person who recites that *berachah* joyously will merit descendants who reflect his enthusiasm.

The Baal HaTanya speaks of the joy in learning Torah that surpasses other joys.

Rav Yechezkel Abramsky and his family lived in London during the years of World War II. Their apartment was on the second floor of a building whose lower floor was rented out to Lloyd's of London, a prominent British bank. When London came under air attack from German fighter planes, residents of the building hurried down to the bomb shelter, which was in the bank's underground vault. The Abramsky family would join their fellow residents and the bank's employees in a large, heavily protected room, the walls lined with safety deposit boxes.

Each of these boxes contained piles of cash, precious stones, and priceless family heirlooms.

The Rav had a private library in the shelter, comprised of a small Chorev Shas, and it was in that corner of the vault that he wrote the Chazon Yechezkel on Rosh Hashanah and Yoma, sirens wailing and frightened people all around him as his pen skipped over the paper.

And each time he entered that room, he would whisper a few words with great emotion. His family leaned in to hear what they were, and they realized what he was saying. טוֹב לִי תוֹרַת פִּיךָ מֵאַלְפֵי זָהָב וָכָסֶף, *"Your Torah is more precious to me than thousands in gold and silver" (Tehillim 119:72).*

Yes, he was saying, I am in a room filled with valuable and costly diamonds, surrounded by gold and silver — but my sefarim and papers are the true valuables in the vault.

The greatest treasure of all is not one that can be felt by the human hand, and it cannot be bought or sold; rather, it is accessible to all, and it can elevate and refine the human soul, imbuing it with fulfillment and delight.

As the Baal HaTanya writes, "It is a joy that surpasses his joy over all the pleasures of the world."

The *Mishnah Berurah* (47:2) quotes this Gemara as well and explains what *Chazal* referred to when they said that Klal Yisrael did not recite the *berachah* on the Torah before learning. "For even though they learned Torah, they didn't immerse themselves in it for the sake of *limud haTorah*, but just as if they were learning any other stream of wisdom. This is what is meant that they did not 'bless the Torah first.' It wasn't more important in their eyes than any other science or discipline."

A Jewish professor in one of the respected universities in California would visit the Los Angeles yeshivah headed by Rav Simcha Wasserman, in order to recite Kaddish. The Rosh Yeshivah greeted him pleasantly and with time, the academic formed a connection with Rav Simcha.

Eventually, he felt comfortable enough to ask the Rosh Yeshivah a question.

"We are both teachers," the professor began. "You impart knowledge and I impart knowledge. What is the essential difference between us? The Torah you teach is a stream of wisdom and the advanced math I teach is also a stream of wisdom. Why do you consider yourself to somehow be doing something better, or more elevated than what I do, when it's really the same thing?"

Gently, Rav Simcha asked the gentleman how many students he had. The professor replied that he'd taught hundreds of students over the years, perhaps even thousands.

"Would you say you had a good relationship with them?" asked the Rosh Yeshivah.

"A wonderful relationship," the gentleman answered.

"How many of those students have invited you to their weddings?" Rav Simcha asked.

The professor looked at him in surprise. "To their weddings? Why would they invite me to their weddings? I'm their teacher, not their friend."

Rav Simcha smiled. "By us, a student would never consider getting married without the teacher. We don't give them information, but life itself. The substance of what we teach is eternal, and so the relationship is eternal too! That is the difference."

לַעֲסוֹק בְּדִבְרֵי תוֹרָה —
To engross ourselves in the words of Torah.

The word *eisek* refers to business dealings. Unlike a clerk, who has the luxury of forgetting about his job once the store is

וְהַעֲרֶב נָא יהוה אֱלֹהֵינוּ אֶת דִּבְרֵי תוֹרָתְךָ
בְּפִינוּ וּבְפִי עַמְּךָ בֵּית יִשְׂרָאֵל. וְנִהְיֶה אֲנַחְנוּ

closed for the night, the business owner is constantly thinking about his company, his mind focused on the bottom line.

Limud haTorah is not a job, or even an occupation: it is a preoccupation.

Rav Shraga Feivel Mendlowitz would often tell his *talmidim* that he learned true *hasmadah,* diligence, from Rav Aharon Kotler. They had participated in a serious *klal* meeting together, and weighty subjects had been discussed. Rav Aharon had been very involved in the deliberations, speaking with his usual clarity and passion. They left the office where the meeting was held, heading to the elevator, and Rav Shraga Feivel heard Rav Aharon say to himself, "Ahhhh... now one can understand Rav Akiva Eiger's *kushya...*"

That, Rav Shraga Feivel would say, is a picture of one who is completely immersed in learning at all times.

> Just after the 1967 liberation of the Old City of Yerushalayim, Jews came pouring into its holy alleyways from all across the country. Many of them were desperate to see and touch the Kosel, while others, who had lived in the neighborhood before 1948, were eager to see their old homes. The narrow streets were crowded, and local Arab shopkeepers responded to the crowds, setting up tables with all sorts of trinkets for sale.
>
> A group of talmidei chachamim from Bnei Brak made the trip as well, Rav Dov Landau, the Slabodka Rosh Yeshivah, among them. Rather than hastening to approach the Kosel, he stopped near the Arab vendors and was soon deeply engaged in conversation with a group of merchants. His friends looked on in wonder; his motive soon became clear.

Sweeten, please, HASHEM, our God, the words of Your Torah in our mouth and in the mouth of Your people, the House of Israel. May we

> *Rav Dov had come with a mission, bearing several obscure Arabic words that the Rambam uses in Peirush HaMishnayos that needed translation — and he had finally found people who could help him!*
>
> *This was his goal: a little more clarity in Torah, a better understanding of a Rambam.*

There is nothing else. It's an *eisek*, a preoccupation that consumes the one fortunate to become one with Torah.

וְהַעֲרֶב נָא —
Sweeten, please.

Generally, when the Torah uses the phrase "milk and honey," the *pasuk* lists milk before honey — as in אֶרֶץ זָבַת חָלָב וּדְבָשׁ. Milk is a basic nutrient, necessary for a person to flourish and thrive, while honey is a sweet, pleasant treat, but not essential for growth. Milk, therefore, is given precedence.

There is one exception: The *pasuk* says: דְּבַשׁ וְחָלָב תַּחַת לְשׁוֹנֵךְ, *Honey and milk are under your tongue* (*Shir HaShirim* 4:11). Here, honey is written first — because this *pasuk* is about learning Torah, and when it comes to learning Torah, the sweetness is essential, not an additional benefit but the core.

Torah, explains Rav Yisroel Reisman, is sweet not because of any additives, but because of its very essence, and so in this *pasuk* the honey is listed even before the milk.

> *A certain bachur was struggling in yeshivah and when his rebbi sat down to discuss it with him, the young man voiced his opinion that if an audience could be arranged with Rav Aharon Leib Shteinman, it would help him greatly.*
>
> *The rebbi arranged an appointment for the boy, but*

the boy made a deal. "Rebbi can come with me, but rebbi cannot stop me from asking the Rosh Yeshivah the questions I want to ask."

The scheduled time came and together, rebbi and talmid entered the humble apartment at Chazon Ish 5 for their meeting with the gadol hador.

Rav Shteinman welcomed them and the boy immediately asked his first question. "Does the Rosh Yeshivah enjoy steak?"

Rav Shteinman wasn't sure what the boy meant, and he said so. "I don't know what that is."

Even as the rebbi looked on in surprise, the boy forged on. "It's the choicest cut of meat, it's expensive and delicious."

Rav Shteinman shook his head. "No, I don't think I have ever tasted it."

"But Rosh Yeshivah," the boy persisted, "how can that be? Everyone says it's so delicious and people pay lots of money for a good piece of steak."

Rav Shteinman was quiet, unsure of what the young man wanted.

"Rosh Yeshivah, please answer me… how can the Rosh Yeshivah say he doesn't like it if everyone else says it's tasty?"

The boy's rebbi was growing more uncomfortable by the moment, but he'd promised not to intervene and he kept his word.

"I simply don't enjoy these things, that's the reality," Rav Aharon Leib answered.

"Well, Rosh Yeshivah" the bachur burst out, "ever since I've been very young, everyone keeps saying that Torah is so geshmak, Torah is so sweet, Torah is so enjoyable… well, guess what, I don't enjoy it! My reality is that I don't find it sweet, no matter what they say!"

It was quiet in the little room as the Rosh Yeshivah and the humbled rebbi understood where the boy had been headed — and the source of his pain.

Rav Aharon Leib thought for a moment, then asked the boy a question.

"Do you find honey to be sweet?"

"Yes," said the bochur, "I do."

"I do as well," said the Rosh Yeshivah, "so we both agree that honey is sweet. Now what would you say if someone told you that honey isn't sweet?"

The boy didn't hesitate. "I would say he's wrong."

"Exactly," said Rav Aharon Leib. "If someone argues that honey isn't sweet, there is only one conclusion: that person has a sore in his mouth that prevents him from tasting the honey, so the natural effect of honey isn't being felt."

Rav Aharon Leib spoke gently to his young visitor. "There are so many blocks, impediments that can prevent the neshamah from experiencing the sweetness of Torah, but that doesn't mean that Torah isn't sweet… it just means a person has to remove those impediments and taste just how delicious it is. The sweetness is there."

It creates a joy that is easily visible on the face of the lomeid Torah.

❧

Rav Nosson Tzvi Finkel would often recall a particular moment, an image that had seared itself upon his soul and filled him with the extraordinary ahavas Torah that would define him.

The Chicago teenager had accompanied his parents on a routine visit to Eretz Yisrael, where they had visited with his great-uncle, Rav Eliezer Yehuda Finkel, the Mirrer Rosh Yeshivah. Though Nosson Tzvi was a fine, polite boy, he wasn't envisioned as a candidate to stand at the helm of the yeshivah world — but his great-uncle was clearly enamored of him, and the Rosh Yeshivah insisted that the young man be sent to Eretz Yisrael after graduating high school.

It might not have been their plan, but Nosson Tzvi's parents agreed and, at the age of sixteen, the American

וְצֶאֱצָאֵינוּ [וְצֶאֱצָאֵי צֶאֱצָאֵינוּ] וְצֶאֱצָאֵי עַמְּךָ בֵּית יִשְׂרָאֵל, כֻּלָּנוּ יוֹדְעֵי שְׁמֶךָ וְלוֹמְדֵי תוֹרָתֶךָ לִשְׁמָהּ. בָּרוּךְ אַתָּה יהוה, הַמְלַמֵּד תּוֹרָה לְעַמּוֹ יִשְׂרָאֵל.

בָּרוּךְ אַתָּה יהוה אֱלֹהֵינוּ מֶלֶךְ הָעוֹלָם, אֲשֶׁר בָּחַר בָּנוּ מִכָּל הָעַמִּים וְנָתַן לָנוּ אֶת תּוֹרָתוֹ. בָּרוּךְ אַתָּה יהוה, נוֹתֵן הַתּוֹרָה.

youth was sent to the Mir. He was welcomed to the home of the Rosh Yeshivah, his bed set up in Rav Leizer Yudel's living room.

At about 4 o'clock the next morning, the newcomer heard noises in the room, and he opened his eyes to see his revered host approaching the sefarim shelf. Unaware that the visitor was watching him, Rav Leizer Yudel walked over to the set of Shas and spread his arms around it for a long moment, embracing as many sefarim as he could grasp at once.

He closed his eyes, then kissed the volumes — and then, he started to slowly recite Birchos HaTorah with great feeling.

Nosson Tzvi saw this, and he connected with the love coursing through that room in a deep way, internalizing it and making it his own. That love, ignited by his uncle's Birchos HaTorah, would flow forth from him, creating a yam haTorah, an ocean that would one day encompass thousands of bnei Torah.

אֲנַחְנוּ וְצֶאֱצָאֵינוּ — We and our offspring.

The *mefarshim* wonder why the term צֶאֱצָאֵינוּ, *our offspring*, is used, and not the usual בָּנֵינוּ, *our children*?

and our offspring [and the offsprings of our offsprings] and the offspring of Your people, the House of Israel — all of us — know Your Name and study Your Torah for its own sake. Blessed are You, HASHEM, Who teaches Torah to His people Israel.

Blessed are You, HASHEM, our God, King of the universe, Who selected us from all the peoples and gave us His Torah. Blessed are You, HASHEM, Giver of the Torah.

Banim, our children, refers to the fact that *we* are the catalyst for *their* existence. *Banim* is derived from the word *binyan*, building, for we have spawned the next generation. *Tze'etza'im* refers to their being a continuation of our own essence and existence. The word *tze'etzah* is derived from *yetziah*, like the outward flow of a river, a continuum that derives from a source, and speaks of their role and mission for the future.

Since the *berachah* begins with the request for אֲנַחְנוּ, *we,* the request for our children is not a separate plea for our children, but rather, the ultimate gauge of how deep our connection is with the Torah: May our engagement in Torah and knowledge of Hashem be such that it creates a never-ending stream of living waters, flowing forward through the generations.

Who — אֲשֶׁר בָּחַר בָּנוּ מִכָּל הָעַמִּים וְנָתַן לָנוּ אֶת תּוֹרָתוֹ *selected us from all the peoples and gave us His Torah.*

The *Tur* (*Orach Chaim* 47) tells us that the "choice" Hashem made refers to Har Sinai, when we were chosen from all the other nations and given the Torah.

This is puzzling, because *Chazal* (*Avodah Zarah* 2b) tell us that

Hakadosh Baruch Hu circulated among the nations of the world, offering each one the Torah. Every nation had its own reason to reject it, until Hashem came to Yisrael, who accepted it.

If we were the last to be offered this gift, how can we say that Hashem chose us? There was simply no one else to ask!

The Chasam Sofer answers this by comparing it to a father of several sons. Only one of them follows the father's ways and brings him joy, while the others do the opposite. The father knows his time on earth will soon end, and he wishes to divide the inheritance among them without causing dissent by giving one a greater portion than the others.

But he also wants the worthiest son to receive a greater share, and he conceives of a plan. He takes the worthy son aside and teaches him a new skill: how to identify precious stones, even when they don't appear to have any value at all. Then the father teaches him how to polish them so that their true value can be realized.

Once the son has mastered the art of discerning value and being able to reveal it, the father calls his sons together and informs them that he is dividing up his holdings between them, offering each one to choose that which they desire.

There are lush fields, large buildings, and attractive gardens. Each of the sons selects a property, and the worthy son takes that which no one else wants — a rock-strewn, unattractive field that seems impossible to cultivate.

They see rocks, but he sees the potential for great wealth, for he knows that if he invests hard work, these rocks will be revealed as valuable treasures.

The Torah appears difficult, but to one with vision and acuity, the potential for real value is obvious. Hard work yields an extraordinary treasure. The other nations saw the rock-strewn field, and Klal Yisrael saw a cache of precious stones.

How did we know? This is because Hakadosh Boruch Hu implanted within us an instinctive insight, the sensitivity that would enable us to discern the value, and the drive that would allow us to toil and uncover it.

He chose us!

When a person approaches the Torah, he recites a *bera-chah* before his *aliyah* and another when it is completed. The two *berachos,* explains the Sfas Emes, are comparable to the two *berachos* recited on food, one before eating and one after the meal is complete. *Bircas HaMazon* can be recited until "*shiur ikkul,*" until the food has been digested, for it is until then that a person feels the satisfaction of having enjoyed a meal, and the second *berachah* is for that pleasure.

Torah, says the Sfas Emes, becomes a part of the person, the words and concepts an integral part of his essence.

Chassidim told the Kotzker Rebbe, Rav Menachem Mendel Morgenstern, about a young man who had completed all of Shas. "Ehr hut gelernt di gantze Torah," someone said. "He learned all of Torah."

"Yes," replied the Rebbe, "ubber voss hut di Torah eim gel-ernt, what did the Torah teach him?"

❧◈❧

The connection between *Birchos HaTorah* and the first prayers of the new day is revealed in a powerful story retold by the Barniver Rav, a close chassid of the Divrei Chaim of Sanz, Rav Chaim Halberstam.

> *One morning, this distinguished chassid was watching as the Rebbe arose from his very brief slumber. The Rebbe started to recite Modeh Ani, saying the words slowly, again and again — Modeh Ani lefanecha, Modeh Ani lefanecha, Modeh Ani lefanecha... the Divrei Chaim repeated the words, clearly feeling that he wasn't expressing that which he aspired to.*
>
> *Finally, the Rebbe sighed deeply and stopped trying, asking for a Gemara. He said Birchos HaTorah and immersed himself in learning, spending two hours plumbing the depths of the Gemara in front of him.*
>
> *Then he gently closed the Gemara, and with his features alight and his voice filled with enthusiasm, he called out, "Now I know Who the Melech is and I can thank Him properly... Melech chai v'kayam!"*

יְבָרֶכְךָ יהוה וְיִשְׁמְרֶךָ. יָאֵר יהוה פָּנָיו אֵלֶיךָ
וִיחֻנֶּךָ. יִשָּׂא יהוה פָּנָיו אֵלֶיךָ, וְיָשֵׂם לְךָ
שָׁלוֹם.[1]

❧❀❧

Words of Torah — both Chumash and Mishnah —
are recited immediately following Birchos HaTorah,
so that words of Torah follow the berachah recited on
Torah. This ensures that a person begins the day with
learning Torah — which, as we see in this Mishnah, "is
equivalent to all [the mitzvos]."

"And the scholars of France had the custom of reciting the
pesukim of Torah, then *Eilu devarim*, which is a Mishnah, and
Eilu devarim she'adam ochel, which is a Baraisa, in order to
fulfill the dictum of the Yerushalmi that one should learn Torah
right away" (*Tosafos, Berachos* 11b).

יְבָרֶכְךָ ה' וְיִשְׁמְרֶךָ. יָאֵר ה' פָּנָיו אֵלֶיךָ
וִיחֻנֶּךָ. יִשָּׂא ה' פָּנָיו אֵלֶיךָ וְיָשֵׂם לְךָ שָׁלוֹם —
May Hashem bless you and safeguard you.
May Hashem illuminate His countenance for you
and be gracious to you. May Hashem turn His
countenance to you and establish peace for you.

Why is *Bircas Kohanim* chosen as the segment of Torah
with which we begin the new day?

The *Beis Yosef* (*Orach Chaim* 48:2) suggests that we recite
these *pesukim* because the *anshei mishmar* (the group of
Kohanim charged with serving in the Beis HaMikdash that
week) said them each morning, as a way of blessing their
fellow Kohanim.

The Avudraham teaches us that we specifically recite these
pesukim in order to recall the blessings bestowed upon Klal
Yisrael.

May HASHEM bless you and safeguard you. May HASHEM illuminate His countenance for you and be gracious to you. May HASHEM turn His countenance to you and establish peace for you.[1]

_____

(1) *Bamidbar* 6:24-26.

> *The last Rebbe of Radomsk, Rav Shlomo Chanoch HaKohen Rabinowitz, Hashem yinkom damo, had a chassid who was a successful businessman. This chassid was involved in a complicated deal with the chassid of another Rebbe, and the deal ultimately turned sour, leaving them engaged in a din Torah. The second chassid threatened the Radomsker chassid that if he would not give in, he would have his Rebbe curse the Radomsker chassid.*
>
> *The Radomsker chassid was frightened and he hurried to Sosnowiece, to the court of his own Rebbe. He explained the situation and asked his Rebbe to issue a curse of his own, to counter that of his former partner.*
>
> *The Radomsker Rebbe smiled gently. "I do not know how to curse," he responded, "but I am a Kohen and I can do something much more powerful. I am able to bless…"*

The *Mishnah Berurah* (47:20) adds that we choose these *pesukim* because they are a series of three *pesukim* in a row, the minimum number necessary for one to receive an *aliyah* to the Torah.

But perhaps there is a message here, unique to the new day, as well.

The last Mishnah in Mishnayos states: לֹא מָצָא הַקָּדוֹשׁ בָּרוּךְ כְּלִי מַחֲזִיק בְּרָכָה אֶלָּא הַשָּׁלוֹם, *Hakadosh Baruch Hu did not find a vessel that contains blessing, other than peace* (*Uktzin* 3:12).

What is meant by the fact that *shalom* is a vessel that contains blessing?

אֵלּוּ דְבָרִים שֶׁאֵין לָהֶם שָׁעוּר: הַפֵּאָה וְהַבִּכּוּרִים וְהָרֵאָיוֹן וּגְמִילוּת חֲסָדִים וְתַלְמוּד תּוֹרָה.

In life, people are given gifts. Money, children, talents, enthusiasm, friends — these are all special gifts, but how a person will use the gifts given to him depends on his agenda and what he hopes to accomplish.

When people are focused on constructive actions, they invest all their energies in building, but if they are involved in a fight, intent on winning, then all those gifts, the talent or money or influence, are put to use toward that end.

Their money and talents become weapons of war.

In that case, these blessings aren't blessings at all but the opposite, agents of destruction.

Hakadosh Baruch Hu showers us with *berachos*, but what then? How do we ensure that they remain blessings? For that, He gives us a vessel that will ensure that they remain *berachos*, and that vessel is *shalom*. Because a person at peace will put every gift available to the proper use.

This is why "*shalom*" is the concluding *berachah* in *Bircas Kohanim*. Once the *berachos* for children, money, and Divine illumination come flowing down, we need one more thing to keep them intact — *Shalom*.

This is a message at the start of a new day. Take the gifts Hashem has bequeathed you and use them to accomplish, rather than the opposite.

— אֵלּוּ דְבָרִים שֶׁאֵין לָהֶם שָׁעוּר: הַפֵּאָה וְהַבִּכּוּרִים
These are the precepts that have no prescribed measure: the corner of a field [which must be left for the poor], the first-fruit offering...

The Sfas Emes suggests that there is a lesson here especially appropriate for the start of a new day. *Bikkurim*, the

These are the precepts that have no prescribed measure: the corner of a field [which must be left for the poor], the first-fruit offering, the pilgrimage, acts of kindness, and Torah study.

first-fruits, represent the start of the process, the moment of beginning. *Pe'ah*, that which is left over from the harvest in the corner of the field, represents the conclusion of that very same process, the ending.

We recite *Birchos HaTorah* and we express the hope that the Torah will fill our day, when we sit and when we go, when we remain home and when we travel, our thoughts will be saturated with Torah.

To one blessed with insight and perception, the values of the Torah apply to every single situation in life, and there isn't an action or decision a person makes that doesn't, on some level, reflect the Torah's light.

The Skulener Rebbe, Rav Eliezer Zusya Portugal, moved into a new home and he called an electrician to do work for him. The Rebbe didn't have any renovations in mind, and the décor and layout were unimportant; there was but a single change he wanted to be done.

The light switch for the washroom was on the inside, and the Rebbe wanted the electrician to move the switch to the hallway outside, if it was possible. The electrician assured the Rebbe that it was quite simple, and he went to do the job.

When it was complete, the Rebbe was clearly ecstatic, and he showered the handyman with berachos, along with paying him. Before leaving, the electrician asked if he might be able to hear why this was so important to the Rebbe.

"I will tell you," the Skulener Rebbe said, "it's very simple. I try hard to train myself to see every action

as a mitzvah, because every action is essentially a mitzvah. Every step a person takes can be a mitzvah if his intentions are pure, and every bite of food is a mitzvah as well. Before closing lights in a room, I always think to myself that I am acting to save money, because the Torah values 'Yiddishe gelt,' money that can be used for Torah, chessed, and tzedakah. But inside the washroom, one isn't permitted such holy thoughts, so I had a dilemma: How could I close the switch without the proper thoughts? But how could I think those thoughts in an impure area? But now," the Rebbe's face brightened, *"now you have solved my problem, and I can close the lights from outside, with the right kavannos."*

From *bikkurim* to *pe'ah,* every part of the Jew's day is holy. With this reminder, we begin a new day.

אֵלוּ דְבָרִים שֶׁאֵין לָהֶם שִׁעוּר... וְתַלְמוּד תּוֹרָה —
These are the precepts that have no prescribed measure... and the study of Torah.

The Vilna Gaon in his *peirush* on Mishnayos, *Shenos Eliyahu* (*Pe'ah* 1:1), writes that learning Torah has no minimum *shiur,* and each word is its own separate mitzvah. Therefore, if a person learns a single word of Torah, he gets *schar,* reward, for the mitzvah of *talmud Torah.*

If one word of Torah is a mitzvah, the Gaon concludes, then imagine the value of a page of Gemara, a full *blatt,* with hundreds of words.

Reb Sruly Bornstein connected this teaching of the Vilna Gaon with a story shared by the famed maggid, Rav Yankel Galinsky, in his *hesped* on the Steipler Gaon.

Rav Galinsky was very close with the Steipler Gaon, and he opened up his treasure-house of memories.

He recalled a bachur who was struggling mightily in yeshivah. The bachur felt that he'd tried, but he hadn't tasted success. Chazal, as Rashi in Chumash

(Bamidbar 8:24) quotes, teach that "A pupil who does not see any success in his study during five years will never see it."

The bachur and his rebbi went together to speak with the Steipler Gaon, feeling that this young man, who had tried and found no success, was absolved of the requirement to remain in yeshivah.

They wrote down their question and the Steipler Gaon reviewed it.

"You had no hatzlachah in yeshivah?" the elderly gadol asked the bachur.

The bachur shook his head. No. He'd tried, but it was clear to him that he simply wasn't cut out for learning.

"Did you learn a masechta of Gemara over the last five years?" the Gaon asked.

Again, the bachur shook his head. He hadn't.

"What about a masechta of Mishnayos?" the gadol asked.

This time, the bachur nodded. He had learned some Mishnayos in yeshivah.

"Five years ago, when you started in yeshivah, had you learned a masechta of Mishnayos?" the Steipler Gaon asked.

No, the bachur conceded, at that point, he hadn't yet learned Mishnayos.

The Steipler Gaon looked at the rebbi in alarm. "This is called someone who did not see berachah in his learning? This is someone you would allow to leave the beis medrash? Five years ago he couldn't learn Mishnayos, and look at him now! He can learn a mishnah! That's not success?"

We tend to value only large accomplishments, easily impressed by numbers and statistics. The Gaon is teaching us that every single word of Torah is precious, and a day upon which one learned Torah — even one word — is a day filled with meaning.

אֵלּוּ דְבָרִים שֶׁאָדָם אוֹכֵל פֵּרוֹתֵיהֶם בָּעוֹלָם הַזֶּה וְהַקֶּרֶן קַיֶּמֶת לוֹ לָעוֹלָם הַבָּא. וְאֵלּוּ הֵן: כִּבּוּד אָב וָאֵם, וּגְמִילוּת חֲסָדִים, וְהַשְׁכָּמַת בֵּית הַמִּדְרָשׁ שַׁחֲרִית וְעַרְבִית, וְהַכְנָסַת אוֹרְחִים, וּבִקּוּר חוֹלִים,

כִּבּוּד אָב וָאֵם —
The honor due to father and mother.

Rebbetzin Yosfa Barzam entered the home of her father, the Steipler Gaon, one day, and informed him that Reb Chaim was suffering from back pain. He immediately reached for his hat and headed out, walking directly to the nearby home of his son, Rav Chaim Kanievsky.

The Steipler Gaon, acquainted with various remedies, was intent on easing the pain of his son so that Rav Chaim Kanievsky could continue to learn Torah without distraction. He entered Rav Chaim's home and directed his son to lie down and lift his shirt.

Rav Chaim complied. His father removed a vial of oil from the pocket of his frock and began to administer the oil to Rav Chaim's back. After several minutes, he suggested that his son lie there and rest for a while. "Then you will feel all better, im yirtzeh Hashem," the Steipler said.

He returned home and told his family that he had gone to Rav Chaim to help with the pain. Rebbetzin Barzam looked at her father in alarm. "I didn't mean my brother Rav Chaim, but my son-in-law Rav Chaim Kluft. He is the one suffering from back pain."

The Steipler Gaon hurried back to his son's home and found Rav Chaim lying in the very same position, following his father's instructions.

These are the precepts whose fruits a person enjoys in This World but whose principal remains intact [for him] in the World to Come. They are: the honor due to father and mother, acts of kindness, early attendance at the house of study morning and evening, hospitality to guests, visiting the sick,

> He hadn't asked. He hadn't explained. He hadn't wondered. He'd simply followed what his father had told him to do, because whatever his father said was worthy of reverence and awe, whether he understood it or not.
>
> Because kibbud av va'eim means not just to listen to one's parents, but to cherish and revere their every word.

וּבְקוּר חוֹלִים —
Visiting the sick.

Some understand the term בְּקוּר, *bikkur*, based on the usage of the same term in regard to *korbanos*. There is a *din* of *bikkur* before bringing a *korban*, in which the animal must be examined to ensure that there are no blemishes or disqualifying injuries. *Bikkur* means to make sure that the animal is fit to be offered on the *Mizbei'ach*.

So too, *bikkur cholim* would not merely mean a "visit," but an examination of the *choleh*, to see what he needs and make sure those needs are being met.

> The Tosher Rebbe, Rav Meshulam Feish Lowy, was an exalted figure, a man who appeared to live in two worlds at once, eating little, sleeping less, but somehow, completely understanding the realities of the individuals he helped each day.

He would often travel from the hamlet of Tosh to Montreal to visit the sick. These visits entailed not just small talk, but a thorough inspection: How was the patient's family faring financially while he was in bed? Who was taking the children to shul or doing homework with them? Was the medical care adequate?

Once, he went to visit an elderly couple in their home in Montreal. It was deep into the winter, and the stairs to their home were blanketed in thick snow. Inside the home, the Rebbe, who perceived that both the man and his wife were slipping mentally, asked if anyone cared for them. They had an only son in New York, they said, and he took good care of them, they insisted. Did they bathe regularly, the Rebbe asked.

Yes, they confirmed, a nurse came each day to make sure they were clean and that there was food in the house.

The Rebbe listened closely, but didn't say very much. He gave them warm berachos, thanked them for having him, and then left.

That night, he asked the gabbai to place a phone call to the son in New York, and then the Rebbe took the phone. "Your parents need help," the Rebbe said, "someone to come in each day and make sure they are eating, that they are warm and clean. And whatever arrangement is in place now, isn't working."

The son assured the Rebbe that he had a nurse coming in each day.

"Tomorrow morning," the Tosher Rebbe said, "I would like you to fly to Montreal, and we will pay for the ticket. Please do not leave until you have made proper arrangements for them, relying on nothing or no one that you don't see yourself. They need a nurse every single day, and in their poor condition, they think that a nurse comes every single day — but it's not true. No one is coming at all."

The son asked how the Rebbe could be so sure.

"Because," said the Rebbe, a man who seemed to hover in another dimension most of the time, "it hasn't snowed in Montreal in several days, and yet there wasn't a single sign of a footprint in the thick snow on their front steps. No one has come in days."

When it came to *cholim,* the Rebbe was "*mevaker,*" his holy eyes missing not a single detail in making sure it would be good for them.

Bikkur cholim is a form of *gemilus chassadim* not just in that it allows the patient to experience a bit of human company, but in that it can give him a sense of self-worth and desire to keep on living.

A close talmid joined his rebbi, Rav Shlomo Zalman Auerbach — Rosh Yeshivah of Kol Torah and one of the leading poskim of worldwide Jewry — on a visit to the Neve Simcha old-age home. They were going to visit a Jew from the Shaarei Chessed neighborhood, an old, lonely man with few people in the world to ask after him.

They reached the nursing home and headed to the room of this resident, but found him fast asleep. The talmid expected his rebbi to ask the attendant to leave a message, and was shocked when Rav Shlomo Zalman asked the orderly to wake the sleeping man.

The talmid looked at his rebbi in surprise. Wake up a sleeping person?

Rav Shlomo Zalman addressed the unasked question. "He isn't sleeping because he's tired," he explained, "but because he's bored. And if we are here, he won't be bored."

The attendant woke the resident, whose face was suffused with joy once he realized that his "friend" had come to visit. It was clear that Rav Shlomo Zalman had been so eager to chat with him, that the Rav had even asked that he be woken!

וְהַכְנָסַת כַּלָּה, וּלְוָיַת הַמֵּת, וְעִיּוּן תְּפִלָּה, וַהֲבָאַת שָׁלוֹם בֵּין אָדָם לַחֲבֵרוֹ (וּבֵין אִישׁ לְאִשְׁתּוֹ) — וְתַלְמוּד תּוֹרָה כְּנֶגֶד כֻּלָּם.

They enjoyed a delightful conversation, and the talmid, who'd been so impressed with what he'd seen, decided to go on his own to visit this person, who was clearly so lonely.

The elderly man would often repeat the same story to the talmid, the memory of how Rav Shlomo Zalman had woken him up, and always conclude, "Rav Shlomo Zalman iz gevehn azah gutteh, He was such a good person."

Bikkur cholim isn't just showing up, but perceiving the needs of the choleh and how to best lift his spirits.

— וּבִקּוּר חוֹלִים, וְהַכְנָסַת כַּלָּה, וּלְוָיַת הַמֵּת
Visiting the sick, providing for a bride, escorting the dead.

Rav Chaim Kreiswirth, the legendary Rav of Antwerp, Belgium, was famed for his mastery over Shas, his brilliant shiurim, and his masterful oratory. But along with being a pillar of Torah, he was a pillar of chessed as well, investing himself in hearing out the problems of his people and trying to solve each one.

The Rav, blessed with a captivating personality and great warmth, was a prodigious fundraiser, dedicated to hachnassas kallah, particularly those kallahs who had been orphaned. In time, the Rav shared part of his motivation.

He'd been diagnosed with a serious illness and had gone to seek a berachah from Rav Yaakov Yisroel

providing for a bride, escorting the dead, absorption in prayer, bringing peace between man and his fellow, (and between a man and his wife) — and the study of Torah is equivalent to them all.

Kanievsky, the Steipler Gaon, with whom he was particularly close.

The Steipler Gaon indicated this mishnah and wondered why "hachnassas kallah" is listed between bikkur cholim and levayas hameis — shouldn't the mitzvah of accompanying the deceased follow that of visiting the sick?

Perhaps, suggested the gadol, it's because the zechus of hachnassas kallah is sufficient to "come between" the two mitzvos, allowing the sick patient to recover and live a productive, healthy life.

This was the message to Rav Kreiswirth, who devoted himself to raising funds for hachnassas kallah. The Rav of Antwerp remained vigorous and healthy, living to a ripe old age.

— וּלְוָיַת הַמֵּת

Escorting the dead.

One day, Rav Aryeh Levine happened to be walking by the old "Wallach's Hospital," the original site of the Shaarei Zedek Hospital. The back door opened and an orderly wheeled out a bed with a body covered by a sheet, clearly a recent niftar.

Rav Aryeh quickly realized that there was neither family nor friends, not a single person, to pay any sort of respect to the niftar, and he asked the orderly if the deceased was male or female. When he learned that it was a woman, he began to deliver an emotional *hesped about the importance of the Jewish woman, speaking for the few people who happened to be walking by at that moment. Some of them stopped out of respect for Rav Aryeh, and their presence drew others as well; eventually, a small crowd formed. People kept coming, and when he felt it appropriate, Rav Aryeh ended the hesped and began to walk, leading the people along to pay final respects to a meis mitzvah who, moments earlier, had been completely alone.*

Rav Aryeh noticed every single Yid — even when the Yid could no longer notice him.

וְעִיּוּן תְּפִלָּה —
Absorption in prayer.

The Tiferes Shlomo of Radomsk explains that *iyun tefillah*, absorption in prayer, is a form of *gemilus chassadim* because true, heartfelt prayer is a benefit to the entire world and all of humanity. One who truly prays bestows kindness on those around him.

Rav Yitzchok Hutner, the Rosh Yeshivah in Yeshivas Rabbeinu Chaim Berlin, would often speak to his talmidim about the achrayus, sense of responsibility, that is integral to true friendship. He once asked a talmid to become involved with a friend who was in a spiritual crisis. The talmid replied that he'd tried, but he was powerless to help. "There is nothing I can do," the bachur proclaimed.

Rav Hutner replied to his talmid in the form of a letter.

"You say that you are powerless to help... are there no more tears left in your eyes?" the Rosh Yeshivah wrote. "Thankfully, we still believe in the power of a perek of Tehillim when it is recited with a broken heart..."

וְתַלְמוּד תּוֹרָה כְּנֶגֶד כֻּלָּם —
And the study of Torah is equivalent to them all.

The Rambam (*Pe'ah* 1:1) explains that learning Torah leads a person to action; it gives him an understanding of all the mitzvos, including the interpersonal mitzvos. The study of Torah is therefore the catalyst for everything else included in the Mishnah.

The Gemara (*Kiddushin* 40a) refers to the study of Torah as something that benefits both heaven and earth. The Rishonim wonder what benefit the study of Torah by a lone individual is for those around him. Some suggest that it is because the scholar is able to guide others in practical halachah. Rav Chaim Kanievsky connects this with the Gemara (*Pesachim* 68b) in which R' Elazar derives from a *pasuk*, "If not for the study of Torah, the world would not be able to endure."

When a person sits and learns Torah, he is sustaining all of creation, the ultimate act of generosity.

The lay leaders of Radin were gathered at the home of the Chofetz Chaim discussing plans to build a hospital, something the region did not yet have. The wealthier ones pledged to sponsor the costs of hospital beds, this one promising five beds, the other offering ten beds. As the meeting continued, a yeshivah bachur, a talmid of the Chofetz Chaim, entered, hoping to speak to his rebbi.

Obviously annoyed at the interruption, one of the baalebatim scornfully asked, "How many beds is he giving?"

The Chofetz Chaim answered, "Actually, this young man is giving fifty beds to the hospital."

A heavy silence descended upon the room. Could it be? Fifty beds?

The man looked at the bachur with new respect, even deference.

"From where does a bachur have money for fifty beds?" he finally asked.

The Chofetz Chaim looked at him pointedly. "Because when he sits and learns Torah, he drives away illness and pain, bringing berachah to the whole town. His toil is worth fifty beds in the hospital, because it is fifty beds that we do not need."

And the study of Torah is equivalent to them all.

— וְתַלְמוּד תּוֹרָה כְּנֶגֶד כֻּלָּם
And the study of Torah is equivalent to them all.

It was in the early days of Covid-19, a pandemic no one had been prepared for, raging across the world. Along with the panic and despair, the coronavirus forced people into their homes, and just like that, the rite and ritual of vibrant *frum* life halted. The sound of *tefillah b'tzibbur* was stilled, the joyous music of *simchos* silenced, and even the opportunity to share words of *nechamah* with those sitting *shivah* was taken from us.

Everyone was home. Suddenly, there was no more *bikkur cholim* or *levayos,* no more *nichum aveilim* or *simchas chassan v'kallah.* There was nothing.

Even *kibbud av va'eim,* children and grandchildren visiting their parents and grandparents, was suddenly out of reach.

Reb Elan Jaffa was reciting this Mishnah one day during that period and had a profound thought.

And at that moment, as Jews sat in their homes with only their Gemaras as company, the words of the Mishnah rang loud and true.

V'Talmud Torah k'neged kulam. In Torah, you have not just the merits of all the mitzvos, but included in its halachos is the

My God, the soul You placed within me is
pure. You created it, You fashioned it, You

light and radiance of every mitzvah. We could not perform the
mitzvos physically, but we could learn about them, connect
with them, celebrate them through Torah.

It was "*k'neged kulam*," in the sense that it compensated
for all of them.

If you have the Gemara, you have everything.

ↈↈↈ

The *tefillah* of *Elokai Neshamah* does not begin with a *berachah*, or the usual "*Shem U'Malchus*," the acknowledgment of
Hashem's Name and Kingship. Some explain that it is because
Elokai Neshamah is in close proximity to *Asher Yatzar*, which
begins with a *berachah* (and, according to Nusach Ashkenaz,
is recited just before it). The *Beis Yosef* (*Orach Chaim* 214)
explains it differently. Since the theme of the entire *tefillah*
— Hashem's power to create and to blow life into beings, His
ability to grant the *neshamah,* take it back, and then return
it once again — is itself the ultimate in *malchus*, the ultimate
depiction of His complete and total mastery over the universe
and its inhabitants, this would be equivalent to the standard
beginning of a *berachah*.

Elokai Neshamah follows *Asher Yatzar*, says the Vilna Gaon
(*Beur HaGra* 4:61), because just as *Asher Yatzar* gives praise
for the *guf*, the body and its workings, *Elokai Neshamah* is a
prayer of gratitude for the *neshamah*, the soul.

אֱלֹהַי, נְשָׁמָה שֶׁנָּתַתָּ בִּי טְהוֹרָה הִיא —
My God, the soul You placed within me is pure.

The word בִּי, *within me,* refers to the fact that each individual *neshamah* was given to a specific person, suitable for
their unique character and situation: בִּי, it is mine, given to

me and to no other. Why? Because the One Who gave it to me is *Elokai*, my God. He — and only He — knows the unique circumstances of my life. He imbued me with this piece of the Divine because He knows that only I can elevate it, rising above the challenges crafted for me. And therefore — טְהוֹרָה הִיא, it is pure, part of Him, a spark of His faith and confidence in me. My connection with Him, Who placed the soul with me, is unbreakable and alive, the purity of its source defining the *neshamah* forever after.

נְשָׁמָה שֶׁנָּתַתָּ בִּי טְהוֹרָה הִיא, אַתָּה בְרָאתָהּ אַתָּה יְצַרְתָּהּ —
The soul You placed within me is pure.
You created it, You fashioned it.

The *neshamah* was formed and created, and only then implanted in man. Why do we first say טְהוֹרָה הִיא, *It is pure,* and only then refer to the creation and fashioning of the *neshamah*? Shouldn't we recite what happened in order, say-ing, "You created it, You fashioned it... and You placed it in me, it is pure?"

Perhaps this was specifically the point being made by the Anshei Knesses HaGedolah here. This *neshamah* was pure and perfect well before it was created, since it derives from the Source of Purity, and it was then sent down to this world, a spark of the Divine light fashioned by Hashem.

Once created, it was sent down to the lower worlds, even-tually placed within a *guf*, a human body. And from there, from the depths of the universe so far from its source, comes the song. However the person might appear on the outside, and whatever actions or deeds he may have committed, deep within him is a spark of the Divine.

And that? It is *tehorah*! It was pure at the start and it remains pure, always!

טְהוֹרָה הִיא — *It is pure.*

There was a young man from a respected family who veered away from the path of Yiddishkeit. He made his disillusionment with Torah public, and eventually reached a low point, inviting friends from similar backgrounds to a party.

It would be held on the night of Yom Kippur, as the haunting strains of Kol Nidrei would fill shuls and Jewish hearts across the world, and it would take place on a boat. Along with music and dancing, he grilled rabbit meat and served it to his guests.

This young man became engaged to a girl from a respected Torah family and before their marriage, the young woman approached her parents for a blessing. True, she had chosen a different path, but she still wanted to know that they wished her well.

Her father agreed to bless the match on the condition that the couple receive a berachah from Rav Yaakov Meir Schechter, the Rosh Yeshivah of Shaar HaShamayim and one of the leaders of the Breslov community in Yerushalayim.

The young man agreed, but made a condition of his own. There should be no discussion of Yiddishkeit, no attempts to persuade him and his kallah to do teshuvah.

After it was all agreed, an appointment was set and the couple headed to Meah Shearim.

They came into the Rav's study, and the chassan reminded Rav Yaakov Meir that there was to be no discussion of religion and personal choice. Rav Yaakov Meir blessed them warmly, and then said he had just a single question.

"Why rabbit meat?"

The visitor wasn't sure what Rav Yaakov Meir meant and the Rav repeated the question.

"Why did you choose to serve rabbit meat?"

The chassan replied honestly. He was so angry at his Creator, so disenchanted with Yiddishkeit, that he never wanted to return. However, Yom Kippur night posed a problem for him. He would feel a rush of

נִפַחְתָּה בִּי, וְאַתָּה מְשַׁמְּרָהּ בְּקִרְבִּי, וְאַתָּה

longing and severe guilt, and he realized that the only way to completely extinguish those feelings would be to commit an act terrible enough to snuff out that spark. A barbeque on Leil Yom Kippur with that sort of food would completely erase the last vestiges of kedushah within him, he reasoned, and Yom Kippur would no longer fill him with guilt.

Rav Yaakov Meir contemplated his words, then responded. "For sixty, even seventy years, I have been teaching that when people do a mitzvah, they become closer to the Ribbono Shel Olam, and when they do an aveirah, they create distance from the Ribbono Shel Olam. How can you, a person so young, be so smart and have such clear emunah to know this instinctively? It's just amazing."

"Tell me... from where do you get such emunah..."

The young man asked for a moment, and stepped out on the porch, overwhelmed by what he'd just heard. After several minutes, he came back in. "I am home, Rebbe, I am back," he said.

Tehorah hi! Rav Yaakov Meir knew that the neshamah remains pure and unsullied, and that no human has the power or ability to vanquish its holiness. With that confidence, the tzaddik found the right words to awaken the neshamah, a spark that remains forever pure.

אַתָּה נִפַחְתָּה בִּי —
You breathed it into me.

The Zohar HaKadosh teaches us that "Man d'nafach, midilei nafach," One who blows, blows from deep within themselves, their very essence flowing forth.

Man was created through Hashem's speech, while the neshamah of man was derived from Hashem's breath. There is a difference between speaking and blowing outward. A person can speak without interruption for hours, breathing all the while, and he might not feel short of breath. But if a person blows out, even for a short while — like a *baal tokei'a*, for example — he will quickly become exhausted. This is because the breath one blows out comes from deeper within the lungs than the breath emitted when he simply breathes or speaks. This, explains the Baal HaTanya, is the significance of the *neshamah* being generated by Hashem's breath, as if to say that the *neshamah* came from "deeper within" Hashem than the rest of creation, which was formed by Hashem's words.

וְאַתָּה מְשַׁמְּרָהּ בְּקִרְבִּי —
You safeguard it within me.

The *sefarim* teach that the word *"shomer"* means not only to watch, but also to wait, as the *pasuk* says, וְאָבִיו שָׁמַר אֶת הַדָּבָר, *His father awaited the matter (Bereishis* 37:11).

Perhaps in this case, too, we are saying that You, Hashem "await" the *neshamah*, knowing of its infinite potential and glory, waiting for man to justify the gift he carries within him.

> The Beis Yisrael of Ger once approached a bachur and asked him, "What would you say is the greatest praise one can ascribe to the Master of the universe?" The Rebbe stood there waiting for an answer, and the bachur stammered out a few words, unsure what to say.
>
> Finally, the Gerrer Rebbe himself answered. "The greatest attribute of the Ribbono Shel Olam is that He never laughs at a person."
>
> It seemed a cryptic answer, and the bachur wasn't sure what the Rebbe was saying. He went to share the story with the Rosh Yeshivah, Rav Pinchas Menachem, a brother of the Rebbe and eventual Rebbe himself.

עָתִיד לִטְּלָה מִמֶּנִּי, וּלְהַחֲזִירָהּ בִּי לֶעָתִיד
לָבֹא. כָּל זְמַן שֶׁהַנְּשָׁמָה בְקִרְבִּי, מוֹדֶה
אֲנִי לְפָנֶיךָ, יהוה אֱלֹהַי וֵאלֹהֵי אֲבוֹתַי,

The Pnei Menachem heard the story and explained it to the young man by giving a mashal.

Imagine a bachur in yeshivah who never wakes up on time for Shacharis, and the hanhalah threatens to suspend him if it happens again. The bachur promises to change his ways, but the very next day, he misses Shacharis. The mashgiach will have no choice but to follow through and keep his word.

The bachur begs and pleads and earns another chance. The next day, he comes on time to Shacharis, but on the day following, he misses tefillah again and slips into his usual pattern. The mashgiach comes to send him home and the bachur begs for another chance, promising to change. Even a kind mashgiach will laugh inwardly at the argument. The bachur has already made it clear that he will not change!

When we see people trying to change and failing, we grow cynical. Sometimes, the Pnei Menachem continued, the person we doubt is ourselves, laughing at our potential to become bigger.

But not the Ribbono Shel Olam. He believes in us, taking our every step forward seriously, waiting — מְשַׁמְּרָה — for the spark of holiness He planted in us to triumph.

וְאַתָּה עָתִיד לִטְּלָה מִמֶּנִּי, וּלְהַחֲזִירָהּ בִּי לֶעָתִיד לָבֹא —
And eventually You will take it from me,
and restore it to me in Time to Come.

There was a period of time when the Chofetz Chaim rarely left his home. One week, the news spread that

eventually You will take it from me, and restore it to me in Time to Come. As long as the soul is within me, I gratefully thank You, HASHEM, my God and the God of my forefathers,

the Chofetz Chaim would speak very late on the night of Leil Shabbos. The humble home was crowded with talmidim eager to hear their rebbi speak, and in the predawn hours on that Shabbos night, he spoke.

Dawn broke as they sat there, and the Chofetz Chaim began by reciting Birchos HaShachar, the morning blessings, saying each word emphatically. He said Elokai Neshamah, then continued with the berachos, and after he was done he looked around and said, "Gut Shabbos."

That was it. That was the long-awaited shmuess. The talmidim were confused, and one of them finally asked, "Rebbi, was that the whole shmuess? What was the message?"

The Chofetz Chaim repeated the words he'd just said. וְאַתָּה עָתִיד לִטְּלָהּ מִמֶּנִּי וּלְהַחֲזִירָהּ בִּי — And eventually You will take it from me, and restore it to me in Time to Come.

The Chofetz Chaim looked around at his talmidim. "What we are being told here is that just as a person leaves, how he appears when the neshamah is taken from him, that's how he will appear when it is ultimately given back to him. Was he in the midst of growing, or in the midst of falling? Perhaps he was stagnant, comfortable with where he was holding, with no desire to change, at the time he passed away. But this is his reality, and that very neshamah, in whatever state he returned it, will come back to him.

"And so," and here the Chofetz Chaim delivered his shmuess, "live your life in a way that allows your neshamah to shine, for that will be the one that is given back to you in the Time to Come. Let it be a neshamah that will make you proud on that day as well."

כָּל זְמַן שֶׁהַנְּשָׁמָה בְּקִרְבִּי, מוֹדֶה אֲנִי לְפָנֶיךָ — As long as the soul is within me, I gratefully thank You.

During the early years of World War II, Rav Chaim Kreiswirth was confined to the ghetto, Jews all around him being sent to the concentration camps daily. One day, an emaciated Jew shuffled over and made a request of the young talmid chacham.

"Rebbi," he said, "it doesn't look like I am going to last much longer. I can't endure these conditions. Can you take this slip of paper? It is my life savings, money that I sent to a bank account in Switzerland. If you survive these horrible times and manage to get through the nightmare that lies ahead of us, please find my kinderlach and tell them that the money is theirs." Rav Kreiswirth took the piece of paper with the person's name and bank account number and guarded it carefully throughout the war years.

Eventually, the war ended and Rav Kreiswirth settled in Antwerp, where he became the Rav. In addition to being a gaon and a tzaddik, he was an extraordinary baal tzedakah; people constantly came through his house asking for money and help. One day, twenty years after WW II, a visitor from Jerusalem came to his house to solicit funds. Rav Kreiswirth asked for his name, and when the man responded, Rav Kreiswirth froze. He asked the man to repeat his name and then asked where he was from. The man responded that he was born in Europe, but his father had been murdered in the war and his mother had sent him to Eretz Yisrael to live with relatives. He was raised in Eretz Yisrael, where he lived. Rav Kreiswirth asked for more details about the city in which he'd been born, and once satisfied, the Rav went to his safe and removed the worn slip of paper.

He showed the name to the man before him. "Was

this the name of your father?" he asked. Once the visitor confirmed his identity, Rav Kreiswirth showed him the number.

"There is a bank account in Switzerland set up by your father. The money there is all yours." The next day, Rav Kreiswirth made arrangements for a professional financier to accompany the man to get the money. The visitor who had arrived as a meshulach returned home a wealthy man.

This is a story of *emunah,* and a story about the faithfulness and devotion of a *talmid chacham.*

But, added Rav Gamliel Rabinovitch, there is another lesson here as well.

Many people walk around like that collector, begging for money, *when they are actually millionaires — they just don't know where to look*!

If we understood the value of our *neshamos,* Rav Gamliel says, we would realize that not only are we not impoverished — we are wealthier than we ever dreamt!

כָּל זְמַן שֶׁהַנְּשָׁמָה בְקִרְבִּי, מוֹדֶה אֲנִי לְפָנֶיךָ — As long as the soul is within me, I gratefully thank You.

Rav Shach would recount how the gaon and kadosh, Rav Yehoshua Leib Diskin, would visit a certain elderly woman each Erev Yom Kippur, eager to receive her berachos. Rav Yehoshua Leib himself was someone who inspired reverence in others.

Yerushalayimer Yidden wondered what this Bubbeh had done to be so honored by the Saraf, a man they looked at as a fiery angel, and they asked Rav Yehoshua Leib directly.

He shared the background with them.

He had once been walking by her apartment, and in a feeble voice, she called out through the window, "Rebbi, please come give me a berachah.'

Rav Yehoshua Leib went into the humble abode and found the elderly woman, confined to a bed with no

רִבּוֹן כָּל הַמַּעֲשִׂים, אֲדוֹן כָּל הַנְּשָׁמוֹת. בָּרוּךְ
אַתָּה יהוה, הַמַּחֲזִיר נְשָׁמוֹת לִפְגָרִים מֵתִים.
בָּרוּךְ אַתָּה יהוה אֱלֹהֵינוּ מֶלֶךְ הָעוֹלָם, אֲשֶׁר נָתַן
לַשֶּׂכְוִי בִינָה[1] לְהַבְחִין בֵּין יוֹם וּבֵין לָיְלָה.

energy or strength to move. He asked the sick woman what sort of berachah she sought, and she said that she wished for arichas yamim, a long life. It was a surprising answer from an infirm, bedridden woman in a poorly furnished, simple room.

The tzaddik asked her why she wished to extend her days, and she explained. Once each week, a nurse was sent to her home. The nurse would wash her and change the soiled bedding.

"And then, Rebbi, at that moment, when I am completely clean and pure, I am able to make a berachah. In that state, I can recite Hashem's holy Name and that's what makes my life worth living."

This Yerushalayimer woman, who so appreciated the chance to recite a berachah, was the person that the extraordinary tzaddik sought for her berachos.

This elderly woman knew exactly why she was alive, what the point and goal of existence was: All the discomfort and inconvenience of life pales in comparison to the glory of being able to connect with the Master of the universe.

Kol zman, as long as there is a soul within me, I sing.

Morning Blessings — ברכות השחר

The following fifteen *Birchos HaShachar*, morning blessings, acknowledge who we are and what we've been given. We thank Hashem for what He made us, how He made us, and

Master of all works, Lord of all souls. Blessed are You, HASHEM, Who restores souls to dead bodies.

Blessed are You, HASHEM, our God, King of the universe, Who gave the heart understanding[1] to distinguish between day and night.

---

(1) Cf. *Iyov* 38:36.

for the body's process of coming back to life as we embark on the new day.

After each *berachah* is recited, writes the *Yesod V'Shoresh HaAvodah*, a person should take a moment to contemplate and acknowledge and give thanks to the Creator, blessed is He, and only then continue with the next *berachah*.

"For if a person thanks Hashem for providing him with his needs and immediately hurries on to the next *berachah* without any reflection, is that even considered a *berachah* at all? The person moved his lips, but did not give thanks!"

⋘◯⋙

We begin the Birchos HaShachar, the morning blessings, by acknowledging the great gift of understanding. The human mind is complex enough to invent a computer, but there is no computer that can invent a human mind.

אֲשֶׁר נָתַן לַשֶּׂכְוִי בִינָה לְהַבְחִין בֵּין יוֹם וּבֵין לָיְלָה —
Who gave the heart understanding to distinguish between day and night.

The "*sechvi*" refers to the heart of a person, seat of emotional intelligence and insight (*Rosh, Berachos* 60b), but Rashi (ibid.) teaches that in the Arabic language, *sechvi* refers to a rooster. The rooster is not the wisest of animals, but its ability to discern between darkness and light by crowing is wondrous, and we thank Hashem for implanting within us the understanding to

בָּרוּךְ אַתָּה יהוה אֱלֹהֵינוּ מֶלֶךְ הָעוֹלָם, שֶׁלֹּא עָשַׂנִי גּוֹי.

appreciate the ramifications of the rooster's cry.

But why not just thank Hashem directly for the new day itself? Why is it necessary to include the rooster in this *berachah*?

Rav Aryeh Levine explained the unique properties of the rooster. If someone would take a rooster from Yerushalayim to London, would it awaken at dawn in London or at the daybreak of its native Yerushalayim? Rav Aryeh said that the rooster would adapt immediately and awaken at dawn in whatever city it happens to be at the moment. It makes no difference where it was yesterday and where it will be tomorrow; the only reality it knows is today, and it sings the song of today. That's the message of this opening *berachah*. Hashem imbued the rooster with this sense to live in the present and that *berachah* is pertinent to each and every one of us, a way to serve Hashem each and every day.

Once we thank Hashem for the gift of true understanding, which includes the ability to draw distinctions, to be able to differentiate between objects that might appear the same, we continue to the next *berachah*, expressing gratitude for the greatest distinction of all.

მოⴑ

In this berachah, we contemplate our great fortune at having been chosen, created to be part of His holy nation. Not only did He create us in His image, but He has given us 613 Divine commandments with which to connect with Him.

שֶׁלֹּא עָשַׂנִי גּוֹי —
Who did not make me a non-Jew.

Rav Moshe Leib of Sassov once commented that after examining his deeds at the start of a new day, he felt completely

Blessed are You, HASHEM, our God, King of the universe, Who did not make me a non-Jew.

broken, knowing that he was devoid of mitzvos or *zechusim*, merits. But then, he continued, he reached this *berachah* — שֶׁלֹא עָשַׂנִי גּוֹי — and he realized that this attribute was one he did have: He was a Yid, and this awareness filled him with a joy that accompanied him throughout the day. Even before we have performed a single mitzvah, we are already elevated and blessed!

> One morning, the oven in the home of Rav Baruch Ber Leibowitz was being repaired. The workman crouched near the oven, his back to the Kamenitzer Rosh Yeshivah, and toiled to fix the problem.
> Rav Baruch Ber saw the hard work and he thanked the man in Polish, wishing him a pleasant day.
> The repairman stood up and turned to face Rav Baruch Ber, removing his cap and showing his large yarmulka. "A gutten morgen, Rebbi," he said in Yiddish. "It's me, Yankel."
> Rav Baruch Ber immediately apologized for the mistake and Yankel assured the Rosh Yeshivah that he was mochel, he totally forgave him.
> "No," said Rav Baruch Ber, "you can't be mochel yet. Please sit down for a moment."
> The Rosh Yeshivah began to tell the repairman of the glory of a Yiddishe neshamah, how exalted and pure, and the pleasure that Hakadosh Baruch Hu derives from every single mitzvah a Yid performs. For several minutes, Rav Baruch Ber "said shiur," ensuring that the repairman seated across from him clearly grasped precisely what it means to be a Yid.
> "And now," Rav Baruch Ber said, "now you can be

mochel me, now that you understand what I did to you by depriving you of a 'gut morgen Reb Yankel.' Can you be mochel me?"

Rav Shlomo Freifeld, Rosh Yeshivah of Shor Yoshuv, would retell a story highlighting the appreciation that Jews once had for their own sacred legacy.

A Yid in a prewar European shtetl left home for a business trip. He returned a few days later to see the aftermath of a pogrom, houses destroyed, mounds of shattered furniture and overturned tables filling the streets. He hurried to his own home to survey the damage and found that it was completely intact, without even a scratch on the front door.

The houses on either side of his had been wrecked, but his had been spared. He couldn't understand why, and he went inside and asked his family if they knew what caused their house to be left untouched.

Yes, his children replied with obvious pride, they had thought quickly. When they heard the sound of the approaching horde, the bloodthirsty screams, they hurried to decorate the outside of the home with holiday wreaths, so common on the homes of non-Jews at the time of year.

"And when the attackers saw our homemade decoration, they passed right by our house!"

The Yid heard his children's explanation and went to find a hatchet. He started to chop away at the furniture and walls of his home, causing damage on all sides. His wife and children looked at him in alarm — had he lost his mind?

"Better a broken Yiddishe house," he told his family, "than an intact non-Jewish house."

Reb Shlomo would explain the message that this Yid was instilling in his family. Pride in being a Yid is real, and forfeiting that to keep a structure intact is a form of destruction. Of course, there are situations of danger and a Jew must protect his life at all costs, but to this Jew, his house was a small price to pay for the chance to proclaim his pride in being a Yid.

The Bach (*Orach Chaim* 46:11) wonders why we don't thank Hashem "*she'asani Yisrael*," for making me a Yid, in a positive sense, in the style of some of the other *berachos*?

He explains that since *Chazal* concluded that "It would have been preferable had man not been created than to have been created" (*Eruvin* 13b), the *berachah* is not for having made us, but rather, for what sort of soul we were given now that we are here.

Rav Shach offers his own answer to the question. The Ribbono Shel Olam, he explained, made us different and imbued us with attributes of the children of Avraham, Yitzchak, and Yaakov — but what do we do with those gifts? That is up to us. We are charged with "becoming Yidden," making ourselves into Yisrael and living up to the inherent potential in the name.

You're a Yid, is the message, but what sort of Yid will you be? That is up to you.

The Erlauer Rav, Rav Yochanan Sofer of Yerushalayim, would retell how his grandfather, Rav Moshe Sofer (known as the Yad Sofer), had gone to bake matzos during the dark days of 1944, slipping through the streets of Erlau to avoid detection by the Nazi sympathizers on the Hungarian police force.

On his way back, however, Hungarian gendarmes noticed him and quickly arrested him. They pulled him into the local police station and told the officer on duty to "deal with him."

The officer looked his Jewish prey up and down, and with a smirk, he asked, "Tell me, it's bad to be a Jew, is it not?" The Erlauer Rav was silent for a moment, inwardly committing to stand firm and never even articulate the words the officer hoped to hear, even to save his life.

"It is never bad to be a Jew. The Jewish nation is just encountering a bad time," he finally said. The officer looked

בָּרוּךְ אַתָּה יהוה אֱלֹהֵינוּ מֶלֶךְ הָעוֹלָם, שֶׁלֹּא
עָשַׂנִי עָבֶד.

Men say:

בָּרוּךְ אַתָּה יהוה אֱלֹהֵינוּ מֶלֶךְ הָעוֹלָם, שֶׁלֹּא
עָשַׂנִי אִשָּׁה.

up at him in disgust, but didn't react. A few hours later, the
Rav was released. He would repeat the story, reminding his
children and *talmidim*, that never — not in word or even in
thought — did he consider himself anything but fortunate and
blessed to be a Yid.

❧

In the next berachah, we acknowledge our good
fortune in being stamped with the name Yisrael, and
not an eved, a slave. A non-Jewish slave does not
have the intrinsic kedushas Yisrael, even though he
is obligated in most of the mitzvos.

שֶׁלֹּא עָשַׂנִי עָבֶד —
Who did not make me a slave.

Many commentaries explain this *berachah* as a statement
of thanks for the ability and strength to withstand the temp-
tations of the *yetzer hara*: We thank Hashem that we are not
slaves to our desires.

In a *derashah*, Rav Zalman Leib Meisels of Seagate once
explained this *berachah* in very practical terms as well.
"Anyone who can still recall the concentration camps," he
said, "those horrendous years in which Jews toiled for 16,
17, or even 18 hours a day, doing harsh labor under impossible conditions, knows precisely how grateful we have to
be that we are no longer slaves. That was the worst sort
of slavery, and every day that we are not there, we are

Blessed are You, HASHEM, our God, King of the universe, Who did not make me a slave.

Men say:

Blessed are You, HASHEM, our God, King of the universe, Who did not make me a woman.

spared. In our generation, children and grandchildren of those who endured those dreadful years, this *berachah* has new meaning."

ఴఞఴ

While a woman has mitzvos as well, the man is given extra mitzvos, as well as the mandate to learn Torah. In this berachah, we acknowledge the great gift of Torah and mitzvos given to a man.

שֶׁלֹּא עָשַׂנִי אִשָּׁה —
Who did not make me a woman.

There are *mefarshim* who understand this as an expression of gratitude that man does not have to face the daunting challenge faced by women. While a man is charged with performing mitzvos, a woman's role is to safeguard and protect the home. Sarah Imeinu, matriarch of our nation, protected her son Yitzchak from Yishmael, and Rivkah assured that Yaakov would receive the *berachos* from his father. Rochel and Leah turned their back on their father's idols before building their own homes. Each of the four women who would be the founders of our nation rose to the challenge and created homes filled with sanctity and purity for their families.

This is a difficult task today as well, when forces of impurity may wear different faces and names, but are no less threatening. The woman faces a daunting task, and men indicate their recognition of this in this *berachah*.

Women say:

בָּרוּךְ אַתָּה יהוה אֱלֹהֵינוּ מֶלֶךְ הָעוֹלָם, שֶׁעָשַׂנִי כִּרְצוֹנוֹ.

בָּרוּךְ אַתָּה יהוה אֱלֹהֵינוּ מֶלֶךְ הָעוֹלָם, פּוֹקֵחַ עִוְרִים.[2]

שֶׁעָשַׂנִי כִּרְצוֹנוֹ —
Who made me according to His will.

The early commentators teach that the reason behind creation was that Hashem, Who lacks nothing, had a desire to give. *Ratzah l'heitiv l'briyosav.* He desired to actualize His *middah* of *tov*, goodness, through *hatavah*, benefiting others.

A woman is a creature that represents *hatavah*, created in line with His will in creating the world, which is to give. So *she'asani*, she praises Him for creating her, *kirtzono*, according to the will that engendered all of creation.

While men are imbued with a more aggressive nature, women reflect kindness, generosity, and good cheer, close to God's ideal of perfection. Like Him, a woman's nature and desire are to give.

☙◈❧

In the next berachah, along with expressing gratitude for the gift of sight, we reflect upon the wondrous ability we have to open and shut our eyes at will. This berachah encompasses the eyelashes, pupils, corneas, and irises, which allow us vision and show us our world in all its beautiful colors.

פּוֹקֵחַ עִוְרִים —
Who gives sight to the blind.

The *mefarshim* wonder why we give thanks specifically for the eyes, and not the ears or mouth. The *Yesod V'Shoresh*

Women say:

Blessed are You, HASHEM, our God, King of the universe, Who made me according to His will.

Blessed are You, HASHEM, our God, King of the universe, Who gives sight to the blind.[2]

_____

(2) *Tehillim* 146:8.

HaAvodah explains that the gratitude is not just for the eyes, but for the fact that we can open and close them at will, free to decide when to look and when not to look, unlike the senses of smell and hearing, which are usually beyond our control.

The siddur *Oholei Yaakov* also links this with the words of the Divrei Chaim, who taught that the eyes are connected with every part of the head, as evident by the fact that tears will appear in the eyes of a person who eats something sharp. If a person smells something pungent, his eyes will get moist, and similarly, when someone hears something that moves him, tears well up in his eyes, an expression of pain or joy.

This might be why there is such a focus on *shemiras einayim*, guarding the eyes from seeing improper sights: the eyes are the mirror of the soul, reflecting thoughts, tastes, scents, and emotions. They must be protected, treated like the treasures they are.

The *Yesod V'Shoresh HaAvodah* points out that the word פּוֹקֵחַ is in the present tense: Hakadosh Baruch Hu is opening our eyes at every moment. The *Yesod V'Shoresh HaAvodah* suggests closing the eyes while reciting the *berachah,* and then reopening them in order to fully appreciate the magnitude of this ongoing gift.

> The Pnei Menachem of Ger once asked his gabbai to arrange for an appointment with an eye specialist,

בָּרוּךְ אַתָּה יהוה אֱלֹהֵינוּ מֶלֶךְ הָעוֹלָם, מַלְבִּישׁ עֲרֻמִּים.

since when he woke up in the morning, he could not see at all for a few minutes; only after several minutes passed did his vision clear. The gabbai started making calls to locate the best eye specialist and he made an appointment, but a few days later, the Rebbe asked him to cancel the appointment. He had changed his mind and he didn't want to visit a doctor after all.

He explained that since he had to wait for his vision to be restored each morning, he would be that much more aware of what a gift vision is. He didn't want to lose the opportunity he was being given, the chance to be reminded of the great gift constantly.

The Ribbono Shel Olam didn't just give us eyes with which to see: at each moment, He opens them for us, enabling us to behold the wonders of His creation.

కుం

The next berachah expresses gratitude for a person's clothing, garments that keep him warm and comfortable and afford him dignity and pride.

מַלְבִּישׁ עֲרֻמִּים —
Who clothes the naked.

The clothing Hashem provides for us are not mere coverings, but part of our mission in this world. Our garments represent the importance and value we attach to *tznius*, modesty, not mere fashion accessories. *Bigdei Shabbos* and *Yom Tov* take on properties of holiness.

In *Zevachim* (88b) *Chazal* relate how the various vestments of the Kohen Gadol atoned for different sins, each one

Blessed are You, HASHEM, our God, King of the universe, Who clothes the naked.

representative of a different sin. The Kohen Gadol is invested with so much holiness that his clothes reflect that as well, and they too possess spiritual properties.

And even in recent generations, we see that clothing belonging to people of holiness and purity are similarly imbued with *kedushah*, underscoring the relationship between garments and the person they clothe.

> *The Ponevezher Rav would often speak of the elderly Jew he met on a fundraising trip to America, a gentleman who had spent time in the world of European yeshivos as a child before immigrating to America, where he made his fortune.*
>
> *Even though he lived in a city without a strong frum presence, the man was shomer Shabbos and maintained a home connected to Yiddishkeit. He confided in the Ponevezher Rav that really, given his situation, he should have completely assimilated, like many of his friends, but there was something holding him back.*
>
> *As a young boy, he had gone to learn in the great yeshivah in Radin, and he had traveled several days to reach the small town. When he'd finally arrived, he went directly to the home of the Chofetz Chaim to seek admittance to the yeshivah, but the Chofetz Chaim was not home. The Rebbetzin, seeing how exhausted the young boy was, urged him to take a nap, and she prepared a few chairs upon which he could rest. He gratefully accepted the offer and lay down, falling asleep immediately.*
>
> *Soon after, the Chofetz Chaim came home and saw the guest. Concerned that the young boy might be cold, the Chofetz Chaim removed his frock-coat and used it to cover his sleeping visitor.*

בָּרוּךְ אַתָּה יהוה אֱלֹהֵינוּ מֶלֶךְ הָעוֹלָם, מַתִּיר אֲסוּרִים.[3]

"Rebbe, what should I tell you?" the older man completed his tale. "Since that moment, the warmth of the Chofetz Chaim's coat is wrapped around me and I can never really slip away from Yiddishkeit… that coat is holding me close."

Rav Mordechai Weinberg, the late Rosh Yeshivah in Montreal, once remarked that it is not surprising that we find this power ascribed specifically to the frock of the Chofetz Chaim. The *cheit* of *lashon hara* is unique in that it can even leave a mark on the clothing of one who speaks it, *nigei begadim*, the plague of garments, as we find in *Vayikra* (13:47).[1] Now, we have a rule that מִדָּה טוֹבָה מְרוּבָּה מִמִּדַּת פּוּרְעָנוּת, *The measure of Divine good is always greater than that of Divine punishment.* If impurity can create a certain reality, then holiness can certainly achieve that effect.

How fitting that the clothing of this "Kohen Gadol," the Chofetz Chaim, who embodied the ideals of pure speech, would reflect a tangible holiness — since in the realm of speech we find clothing to be impacted!

R' Yochanan would refer to his clothing as "*mechabdosai*, those (things) that honor me" (*Shabbos* 113a), since they bring honor and dignity to the one who wears them.

Rav Mordechai Shlomo Friedman, the Rebbe of Boyan, presided over a *kloiz,* a chassidishe *beis medrash* on the Lower East Side. One year, on Erev Pesach, he was seen in the shul wiping down each bench with a rag, even though the janitor had already cleaned the shul.

A chassid walked in and wondered why the Rebbe was doing this. The Rebbe answered that in the evening, many of

---

1. *Tzaraas,* the punishment for speaking *lashon hara,* also manifests itself on the sinner's garment.

Blessed are You, HASHEM, our God, King of the universe, Who releases the bound.[3]

_____

(3) *Tehillim* 146:7.

the *mispallelim* in shul would be wearing new suits *l'kavod Pesach*. He explained that these suits reflect the stature of a nation of princes, elevated to the point where they are worn to serve Him — the new suits were actually deemed *bigdei malchus*. "I am just making sure that there is no dust or dirt on these benches that might sully these suits."

In the morning, the commentaries relate, along with our physical clothing, we are also gifted with "new suits," the *neshamah* — fresh and restored. In this *berachah*, we contemplate the new beginning and commit to keeping our garments unsullied and pure.

> In the next berachah, we thank Hashem for releasing us from the imprisonment of sleep, allowing us not just freedom of movement, but also the ability to feel revitalized and strong for the new day. We also ask that we remain free of the yetzer hara and his evil designs, because we know that with the new day comes new battles of the spirit.

מַתִּיר אֲסוּרִים —
Who releases the bound.

The well-known maggid, Rav Yaakov Galinsky, was once hospitalized with a painful infection in his legs. At the hospital, they treated the infection aggressively and Rav Yankel found his strength somewhat restored, but he was still in great discomfort. He very much wanted to be home, able to resume his regular schedule of learning and teaching Torah.

בָּרוּךְ אַתָּה יהוה אֱלֹהֵינוּ מֶלֶךְ הָעוֹלָם, זוֹקֵף כְּפוּפִים.

As he lay in his hospital bed, he heard a commotion in the corridor and suddenly, the gadol hador came into the hospital room.

It was Rav Aharon Leib Shteinman, there to visit him!

Rav Yankel quickly sat up straight in deference to his visitor, and Rav Aharon Leib approached.

"Rav Yankel... bist aza gvir, you are such a wealthy man, but I can't tell you exactly how wealthy," Rav Aharon Leib said.

Rav Yankel looked at the Rosh Yeshivah in confusion. "I am wealthy?" he asked.

"Yes," Rav Aharon Leib repeated, "you are very rich, but I don't know precisely how rich."

And he explained. He had just been on a different floor of the same hospital to pay a visit to a respected supporter of Torah, a very successful businessman who was quite ill.

This patient, bedridden and unable to move, told Rav Aharon Leib. "Believe me, Rebbi, I would give away half of my fortune just for the pleasure of being able to get down from the bed and walk across the room... what good is all my money if I cannot even do that? What benefit are all my holdings if I am trapped here, in bed?"

Rav Aharon Leib looked at his friend. "You, Reb Yankel, are able to get out of bed and walk around the room. Did you ever make the cheshbon, did you calculate how much that is worth? Now we know that it is worth at least half of this Yid's fortune, because he told me so. But I don't know the amount of that fortune, which is why I told you that I can't

Blessed are You, HASHEM, our God, King of the universe, Who straightens the bent.

tell you exactly how rich you are — I just know that you are very wealthy…"

Each morning, we thank Hashem for freedom of movement, realizing just how wealthy we are.

ﻌ૭જ৯

In the next berachah, we thank Hashem for differentiating us from animals by enabling us to walk upright. Unlike animals, we were created with our heads erect, reflecting the fact that man is the greatest of all creations, guided by intellect and reason.

זוֹקֵף כְּפוּפִים —
Who straightens the bent.

There is an inherent dignity in the way man walks, his head above the rest of his body, and it symbolizes his potential. Every morning, we arise and stand up tall and straight, reminded that we are created with a "*tzurah*," in the Divine image, with the capacity to emulate Him and to create as well.

Rav Shimshon Pincus was told about an elderly woman, recently arrived in Eretz Yisrael from Russia, who was a granddaughter of the Chofetz Chaim. Determined to meet her and hear whatever he could about the great luminary, Rav Pincus wasted no time in heading to Petach Tikvah, where he visited with the new immigrant.

He asked if she had any memories of her revered grandfather, and the woman, who was not religious, shared a recollection. As a young girl, she said, she was very worldly and sophisticated, having read

בָּרוּךְ אַתָּה יהוה אֱלֹהֵינוּ מֶלֶךְ הָעוֹלָם, רוֹקַע הָאָרֶץ עַל הַמָּיִם.[4]

numerous books. She was conversant in the ideas and doctrines of the political street, and felt herself drawn after the world beyond the yeshivah and the little community of Radin.

Eventually, she made the decision to leave home and attend university, where she was exposed to many foreign concepts. During those years, she had opportunity to visit Radin, and she went to speak with her grandfather.

"Zeide," the eager young girl said, "you have to step out of this dark little world and see the world beyond Radin. It's a new time, and advances in science and technology are creating new realities. You have to let go of the old-fashioned ideas and ideologies and get with the times, see the possibilities that now exist."

"Tochter'l, my daughter," the Chofetz Chaim told her, "the educated ones, with their great advances, will one day reach a point where they will kill thousands of people. They will destroy life. But we, who are holding on to what was... Mir machen mentchen. Zei vellen machen bombes, uhn mir machen mentchen. They will create bombs, but we create people... we create people..."

The world evolves, and technology leaps forward, but we still regard man as the crown of creation, elevated in deed and thought, capable of creating eternity.

A person may be standing before a towering mountain, its peak seeming to reach the sky. He might be overlooking the vast blue ocean, roaring waves crashing at the white sand — but if he is gazing downward, to the ground, he will see only ants crawling across its expanse.

Blessed are You, HASHEM, our God, King of the universe, Who spreads out the earth upon the waters.[4]

(4) Cf. *Tehillim* 136:6.

We thank Hashem, said Rav Sholom Ber of Lubavitch, for creating us with the capacity to see more, to raise our eyes and see His glory, to look upward rather than downward.

The next berachah is the first one in which we look past the kindness performed with man and focus on the kindness inherent in creation itself, beyond the human body. In it, we acknowledge Hashem's might, and also His precision, for water, which has the tendency to move forward, stops at the boundaries He sets for it.

רוֹקַע הָאָרֶץ עַל הַמָּיִם —
Who spreads out the earth upon the waters.

Dry land and water are essentially two competing forces, yet Hakadosh Baruch Hu created a world in which they coexist in perfect harmony.

In *Tehillim* (136:6), the Radak explains that we are praising Hashem for the gift of solid ground beneath our feet. Tragedies of recent years have shown us just how vulnerable we are, with structures considered firm and safe collapsing suddenly without warning.

But Hashem's world endures, firm and solid.

The Gemara (Berachos 60b) teaches us that the next berachah is an expression of thanks for our shoes, which enable us to walk about and take care of our needs. Our shoes and every other need are provided

בָּרוּךְ אַתָּה יהוה אֱלֹהֵינוּ מֶלֶךְ הָעוֹלָם, שֶׁעָשָׂה
לִי כָּל צָרְכִּי.

to us by the Creator. He created the original material and provided the human mind with the inspiration necessary for manufacturing these items.

שֶׁעָשָׂה לִי כָּל צָרְכִּי —
Who has provided me [with] my every need.

Why is this *berachah* recited in *lashon avar*, past tense — שֶׁעָשָׂה rather than שֶׁעוֹשֶׂה?

This is because it has all been taken care of; whatever happens and what will happen is precise, because Hashem has already prepared the road ahead and given me the tools I will need for every situation.

Another difference between this and other *berachos* is the fact that we add the word לִי, *to me*, which we don't find elsewhere. In the other *berachos,* we laud the One Who is פּוֹקֵחַ עִוְרִים, *gives sight to the blind*, or מַלְבִּישׁ עֲרֻמִּים, *clothes the naked.* Here, instead of saying "*oseh tzerachim,*" fulfilling the needs of man, we thank Him for having filled all "my" needs.

Why? Rav Moshe Leib of Sassov explained that the *middah* of *bitachon,* perfect trust, is necessary to survive in a world of darkness and concealment — but it is only when you are the one in a challenging situation that you should have trust. If you see another person who is suffering, then *bitachon* — assuming that since Hashem is in control it will all work out — is not a virtue. Instead, you have to do whatever you can to help, making the other person's problem your own.

This *berachah* hints at that. לִי, for myself, Hashem has done כָּל צָרְכִּי, provided all *my* needs, and I lack nothing; but if my friend is hungry or cold, struggling and in pain, then I have to try to fill that need.

Nusach Sefard reverses the order of the following two blessings.

Blessed are You, HASHEM, our God, King of the universe, Who has provided me [with] my every need.

For me, I can say Hashem has taken care of everything, but for another, I have to be Hashem's agent in helping out and making things right.

Rav Elimelech Biderman told a story he had heard from Rav Yisroel Zicherman, the Rav of Ma'ayanei Hayeshua Hospital. Rav Shmuel Wosner, the Shevet HaLevi, once had to be in the hospital, and the staff and administration lined up to greet the revered Rav.

Rav Zicherman shared a halachic question that a seriously ill patient had asked him earlier in the day. In the throes of a debilitating ailment, the patient couldn't move any of his limbs on his own.

The question he had posed to the hospital's Rav was whether or not he should recite the *berachah* of "*She'asah li kol tzarki*," when it appeared that his most basic needs were not being provided.

Rather than answer the question, Rav Wosner asked if he could visit the patient, and together with Rav Zicherman, he took the elevator to the upper floors.

They entered the room to see a man who could do nothing at all to show his appreciation and respect for the visitor, barely able to lift a finger as a sign of greeting. All the patient could do was move his lips in an attempt at a smile.

"You remind me," Rav Wosner said, "of an incident from many years ago, when my rebbi, Rav Meir Shapiro, took me along when he went to visit a *choleh*, a very ill patient."

The Lubliner Rav entered the room and the patient smiled broadly, a smile that stretched across his entire face.

"Why do you appear so happy?" Rav Meir asked.

The patient explained. "In truth, I should stand up for the Rav when he comes in, I should set out refreshments and prepare a reception as befits such a distinguished guest, but alas, Hakadosh Baruch Hu has taken that from me. I cannot even move a single limb. All I can do, Rebbi, is smile. So if that is all I am able to do, then clearly, that smile is my mission right now, that is why I am here… and if that's the case, I will smile with every ounce of energy I have."

Rav Wosner approached the patient and spoke softly. "I heard your *shailah* in regard to saying the *berachah* of *She'asah li kol tzarki*. I want you to know that your mission is based only on what you are able to do in your situation. That reality defines your *tafkid*, your reason for being here, and since you are doing it, then that is your *'tzarki,'* that's what you need."

Sometimes, it might be just a smile, and other times, it's even less than that — but a person always has the tools to do the job he is meant to do at that moment.

ॐऌऄ

Once we have thanked Hashem for the firm ground beneath our feet, we now express gratitude for the structure of our feet themselves, which enables us to walk with ease. In this berachah, we acknowledge that Hashem plans the pathways through the world He fashioned, assisting us with our every step and leading us to our destinations.

הַמֵּכִין מִצְעֲדֵי גָּבֶר —
Who firms man's footsteps.

One Friday morning, the great gaon Rav Mottel Pogromansky boarded a train and took a seat next to another Jew. Realizing he was in the presence of a distinguished person, the Jew introduced himself to his seatmate and they began to speak.

Blessed are You, HASHEM, our God, King of the universe, Who firms man's footsteps.[5]

(5) Cf. *Tehillim* 37:23.

He worked as a shochet and mohel, he told Reb Mottel as they began to converse in learning. They were quickly immersed in the life-giving wellsprings of Torah, and neither noticed as the train reached their intended destination — and then, after several minutes, pulled out of the train station and continued on to the next stop.

Eventually, the mohel looked through the window and realized that they had missed their stop. Adding to his panic was the fact that they had both been planning to spend Shabbos in the town they had just passed.

"What will we do?" he asked Reb Mottel. "Where will find a place for Shabbos? Where will we get challos and wine? Rebbe, mir zennen farblonzhet, we are so lost!"

Reb Mottel remained calm, assuring his companion that every step a person takes is planned by the Master of the Universe. "A Jew is never lost. Wherever he ends up, that is precisely where he is meant to be."

Reb Mottel brought a rayeh, a proof. On the pasuk (Bereishis 21:14) that relates that Hagar "departed and strayed," Rashi says that she "reverted to the idol-worship of her father's house."

From where does Rashi derive that her leaving indicates a return to idol-worship?

"Because," Reb Mottel explained, "the pasuk says that she strayed, zi hut zich farblonzhet, uhn a Yid farblonzhet zich nit. She was lost, but a Jew is never lost. Wherever they go, it's because they have to be there."

בָּרוּךְ אַתָּה יהוה אֱלֹהֵינוּ מֶלֶךְ הָעוֹלָם, אוֹזֵר יִשְׂרָאֵל בִּגְבוּרָה.

At the next stop, they both got off. It was a small town, and there didn't seem to be any Jews in the hamlet who would welcome them for Shabbos.

Reb Mottel started to ask passersby if they knew of any Yidden, but no one did. The mohel was growing despondent, but again and again, Reb Mottel reassured him that a Jew is never lost, but exactly where he is meant to be.

The sun sank lower in the sky, Shabbos was approaching, and they still had no host. Reb Mottel kept asking, though, and his persistence finally paid off when someone nodded and showed him a hut in the distance. There was a Jew in town!

The two visitors hurried to the small home and knocked at the door.

The door opened and the owner's eyes opened wide, as if he were witnessing a miracle. "You are a mohel, yes?" he asked. The visitor nodded.

The homeowner began to cry, then to laugh and dance as he welcomed his guests.

"Last week," he told them, "my wife gave birth to a boy. Today he is meant to have a bris, but there are no Jews here and certainly no one who can perform the mitzvah of bris milah. I have been davening a whole day, pleading with Hashem that He send me a mohel. And look, you are here, sent by the Ribbono Shel Olam Himself!"

Reb Mottel was sandak for a Jewish child entering the covenant of Avraham Avinu, and he and the mohel spent a beautiful Shabbos with their grateful hosts.

On Motza'ei Shabbos they continued on their way,

Blessed are You, HASHEM, our God, King of the universe, Who girds Israel with strength.

Reb Mottel reminding his new friend that a Jew is never lost.

Wherever he ends up, it is according to a plan, even if human eyes cannot yet see it.

⋘◎◎⋙

In these next two berachos we refer not to man, but to "Yisrael," since the clothing we wear is distinct, marking us as His servants. Included in our thanks is gratitude for designating us with the name Yisrael.

When donning a belt, a person establishes a distinct separation between the upper and lower parts of his body, a divide that helps provide him with the spiritual strength to triumph over the yetzer hara. In this berachah, we thank Hashem for that power, the power to create eternity.

אוֹזֵר יִשְׂרָאֵל בִּגְבוּרָה —
Who girds Israel with strength.

In thanking Hashem for this separation, we are expressing a fundamental truth about the purpose of life. The upper part of our body contains thought, feeling, and speech, while the physical functions are found in the lower regions of the body.

The goal is to use the bodily functions in the lower half to live a life in which the properties of the upper half guide us.

Rav Yaakov Kamenetsky had the opportunity to visit the Philadelphia Yeshivah, founded and led by his son Rav Shmuel. While addressing the *bachurim,* Rav Yaakov discussed the story of Yosef HaTzaddik, a 17-year-old boy in the throes of a land suffused with impurity, far from his sainted father, disdained by his own brothers. If ever a young man had an excuse to succumb to temptation, it was he.

How, then, did Yosef remain strong, rejecting the advances of the noblewoman who wanted to sin with him?

Rav Yaakov shared something he'd heard from an older Jew, a former yeshivah student who had been faced with all sorts of challenges in his life. This Jew told Rav Yaakov that he had the strength to persevere and triumph over those *nisyonos* because in his youth, he had been privileged to see Rav Baruch Ber Leibowitz, the Kamenitzer Rosh Yeshivah. Simply beholding that radiant countenance left an impression on him, arming him with the resources of purity and strength he would need later on.

Chazal (*Sotah* 36b) teach that as Yosef HaTzaddik was engaged in a fierce battle with his *yetzer hara,* he looked to the window and saw his father's saintly image, the face of Yaakov Avinu. What did that face tell him? The face of Yaakov was a plea, a demand, a rallying cry: My son, do not succumb! You are stronger than the temptation, and your strength will one day earn you the merit of having your name on the stones of the *ephod*.

This was Rav Yaakov's message to the *bachurim.* Look at the *kedushah* all around you, soak it in and create a reservoir of holiness so that you will have from where to draw strength throughout your lives.

The Jew knows to look upward, to keep his gaze focused on those people and places that can allow him to live an elevated life, so that when the pull to descend comes, he will be able to withstand it.

∂∂∂

In this berachah, we give thanks for the fact that Hashem rests His presence on our heads, something

Blessed are You, HASHEM, our God, King of the universe, Who crowns Israel with splendor.

He does not do for any other nation. We cover our heads to acknowledge this, something that increases our fear of Heaven.

עוֹטֵר יִשְׂרָאֵל בְּתִפְאָרָה —
Who crowns Israel with splendor.

In thanking Hashem for this crown, we are expressing that our most precious asset is our *seichel*, intellect.

Rav Yosef Zvi Carlebach, the Chief Rabbi of Hamburg, was invited to an extremely upscale event, attended by many leading members of the kehillah — but Rav Carlebach was the only person in the room wearing a yarmulka on his head.

A respected local businessman, somewhat embarrassed by Rav Carlebach's headwear, approached the Rabbi and sarcastically said, "Rabbi, you must be quite warm with such a large covering on your head."

Rav Carlebach smiled genially. "If you appreciate fine wine, my friend, you know that after pouring a glass, you quickly cover the bottle. The reason for this is not just to maintain the taste of the expensive wine, but also to ensure that not a single drop is wasted.

"The same is true of daas, the contents of a person's mind. If each drop of knowledge is precious and valued, then you make sure to keep it covered, eager to protect every priceless drop; but if the head is empty, then there is indeed no reason for a covering."

The Gemara (*Shabbos* 156b) tells us that astrologers told the mother of Rav Nachman bar Yitzchak that her son would be a thief. She heard their prediction and told her son to make sure that his head was never uncovered. The Maharsha

בָּרוּךְ אַתָּה יהוה אֱלֹהֵינוּ מֶלֶךְ הָעוֹלָם, הַנּוֹתֵן לַיָּעֵף כְּחַ.[6]

בָּרוּךְ אַתָּה יהוה אֱלֹהֵינוּ מֶלֶךְ הָעוֹלָם, הַמַּעֲבִיר שֵׁנָה מֵעֵינָי וּתְנוּמָה מֵעַפְעַפָּי.

explains that the astute woman was very zealous with this practice, because she intuited that the increased head covering would lead to increased *yiras Shamayim*.

This *berachah* is an expression of gratitude for that reminder and for the ability Hashem planted within us to be aware of His will at all times.

❦

In the next berachah, we acknowledge the fact that when our neshamah is worn out and exhausted, it is taken from us at night. It is returned in the morning so that we feel revitalized and strong.

הַנּוֹתֵן לַיָּעֵף כְּחַ —
Who gives strength to the weary.

Reb Abba Dunner of London was a respected activist for holy causes, an ambassador for European Torah Jewry and a mentor to many younger askanim.

He endured a very difficult period in his own life, losing his wife and then his beloved son, Reb Bentzi, a renowned baal tzedakah. Then, as he attempted to find the strength to forge on, Reb Abba himself was diagnosed with a dreadful illness.

How, he was asked, did he manage to endure it all with a smile on his face and laughter in his eyes?

It was not easy, he conceded, and there were moments when he faltered. But he shared an eitzah, a piece of advice given to him by the Sassover Rav in London.

Blessed are You, HASHEM, our God, King of the universe, Who gives strength to the weary.[6]

Blessed are You, HASHEM, our God, King of the universe, Who removes sleep from my eyes and slumber from my eyelids. And

(6) *Yeshayah* 40:29.

> The Rav suggested that Reb Abba "adopt" a berachah, one of the daily Birchas HaShachar, and make it his own.
>
> "Develop a deeper understanding of the words and allow yourself to luxuriate over that berachah, taking the time to really feel its meaning," the Rav suggested.
>
> Reb Abba accepted the advice and chose the berachah of "Hanosein laya'ef koach, Who gives strength to the weary," starting off his day by contemplating that Hakadosh Baruch Hu invests tired people — those, like Reb Abba, who might have given in to the pain of challenge and loss — with strength.
>
> And that method was successful, he realized. In time, he started to repeat the words of the berachah several times a day, whenever he felt his strength starting to ebb: contemplating their meaning gave him new energy and he was able to go on.

And those who knew him never even saw the tiredness, just the *koach*, the energy given to him by He Who gives strength to the weary.

৵৹৹৵

> We give thanks to the One Who lifts sleep from our eyes, allowing us to fully awaken, then continue with special requests as one long berachah.

וִיהִי רָצוֹן מִלְּפָנֶיךָ, יְהוָה אֱלֹהֵינוּ וֵאלֹהֵי אֲבוֹתֵינוּ, שֶׁתַּרְגִּילֵנוּ בְּתוֹרָתֶךָ וְדַבְּקֵנוּ בְּמִצְוֹתֶיךָ, וְאַל תְּבִיאֵנוּ לֹא לִידֵי חֵטְא, וְלֹא לִידֵי עֲבֵרָה

הַמַּעֲבִיר שֵׁנָה מֵעֵינַי וּתְנוּמָה מֵעַפְעַפָּי —
*Who removes sleep from my eyes
and slumber from my eyelids.*

Rav Shmuel Unsdorfer explained that the Divine kindness of removing slumber from the eyelids of man isn't worthy of special gratitude unless the person uses his new clarity and vision correctly, "that You accustom us to study Your Torah and attach us to Your commandments."

This idea is reflected in a story retold by Rav Unsdorfer's son, Rav Yaakov Eliyahu Unsdorfer, the revered Rav of Montreal's Mesivta Reishis Chochma and a prominent *mechaber sefarim.*

As a young boy, Rav Yaakov Elya had a throat infection and one morning, he woke up and found that he was having difficulty speaking. He tried, but only a weak sound issued from his mouth. He panicked, and his parents immediately took him to the doctor, but the doctor had no solutions. Over the next few weeks, the concerned parents took him from one specialist to another, from appointment to appointment, but no doctor could help; one respected specialist even predicted that the boy would soon lose his ability to speak completely.

The parents didn't give up, davening with passion and heart while continuing their search for a doctor who could help. In time, they found an expert who agreed to see the boy, making a single condition. The boy was not to speak at all, not even a whisper, until the exam.

Of course, they agreed and waited anxiously

may it be Your will, HASHEM, our God, and the God of our forefathers, that You accustom us to [study] Your Torah and attach us to Your commandments. Do not bring us into the power of error, nor into the power of transgression

for the appointment. They accompanied their son to the prestigious doctor, who examined the boy thoroughly and took several tests. Then he welcomed the parents to his office, assuring them that their son's voice would soon return to its full strength, and that he could immediately resume speaking if he wished. There was no real concern for the boy's speech. He prescribed some medications and wished them well.

As they stepped out into the bright sunshine, the child looked up at his parents, as if requesting permission to begin speaking again. His mother beamed at him, eager to hear his voice, but his father, Rav Shmuel, placed a hand on his shoulder.

"Yaakov Elya," he said, "today is Erev Shabbos. Tonight, we will go to shul for Minchah, and the first thing we will say is kappitel 107 in Tehillim. I want you to try and hold back from speaking just a few more hours, until then.

"And then, my son, then you will open your mouth and cry out the words of tefillah, Hodu laHashem ki tov, ki l'olam chasdo — Give thanks to Hashem for He is good, for His kindness is everlasting.

"Now that you can speak, let those be the first words out of your mouth..."

Rav Shmuel Unsdorfer, a man who saw the gift of speech as a means to praise Hashem, saw the gift of sight given to us each morning as meaningful only when used to see the Torah's truth.

וְעָוֹן, וְלֹא לִידֵי נִסָּיוֹן, וְלֹא לִידֵי בִזָּיוֹן, וְאַל [תַּשְׁלֵט] (יַשְׁלֵט) בָּנוּ יֵצֶר הָרָע. וְהַרְחִיקֵנוּ מֵאָדָם רָע וּמֵחָבֵר רָע. וְדַבְּקֵנוּ בְּיֵצֶר הַטּוֹב וּבְמַעֲשִׂים טוֹבִים, וְכוֹף אֶת יִצְרֵנוּ לְהִשְׁתַּעְבֶּד לָךְ.

— וְלֹא לִידֵי נִסָּיוֹן וְלֹא לִידֵי בִזָּיוֹן
Nor into the power of challenge,
nor into the power of scorn.

Rav Nachman of Breslov explained the connection between *nisayon*, challenge, *and bizayon*, scorn, in a pithy manner, saying, "*Udder a nisayon, udder a bizayon,*" meaning that if one flounders at a time of challenge, this itself is a source of embarrassment.

Often, people endure a challenge that seems too difficult, but then they find the strength to rise above it and realize just how capable they are.

Rav Yitzchok Zilberstein related a story of a courageous Israeli soldier, a young man who rose through the ranks of the military and seemed poised to be promoted into one of the army's top-secret, elite units.

One day, this valiant young soldier was kidnaped by Arab terrorists.

His cruel captors began to press him for information, but the loyal soldier refused to divulge anything. They started to beat him and threaten the well-being of his wife and children, but he wouldn't budge. Much as they afflicted him, he remained firm in his refusal to speak.

One morning, after they had beaten him severely, he fell onto his thin cot, his entire body throbbing with pain. Through the wall, he overheard traces of the conversation between his Arab captors coming

and sin, nor into the power of challenge, nor into the power of scorn. Let not the evil inclination dominate us. Distance us from an evil person and from an evil companion. Attach us to the good inclination and to good deeds and force our evil inclination to be subservient to You.

through the wall, but something made no sense: they were speaking fluent Hebrew.

Suddenly, he grasped that they weren't Arabs at all, but Israelis. He understood that they were fellow members of the Israeli army, sent to test his fortitude.

Once he realized this, he understood that even if there would be more beatings, it was simply part of the test, and they would never actually kill him or harm his family. He felt calm and able to face whatever would come his way, knowing that this was all part of the test they had prepared for him.

They came to pressure him again, but he stood firm, emboldened by the knowledge he carried in his heart, and finally, they told him the truth.

"We are Israelis, posing as Arabs, and we were trying to see how tough you are, if you are capable of joining our elite unit — and you deserve congratulations, because you've earned the promotion," they said.

Ribbono Shel Olam, we ask, don't let us fall to temptation and feel the disgrace of not having passed the test.

וְאַל יִשְׁלֹט בָּנוּ יֵצֶר הָרָע —
Let not the evil inclination dominate us.

The Chofetz Chaim once noticed a group of bachurim sitting and chatting. He approached and asked them what they were talking about, and one of them

וְתִתְּנֵנוּ הַיּוֹם וּבְכָל יוֹם לְחֵן וּלְחֶסֶד וּלְרַחֲמִים בְּעֵינֶיךָ וּבְעֵינֵי כָל רוֹאֵינוּ, וְתִגְמְלֵנוּ חֲסָדִים טוֹבִים. בָּרוּךְ אַתָּה יהוה, גּוֹמֵל חֲסָדִים טוֹבִים לְעַמּוֹ יִשְׂרָאֵל.

earnestly said that they were discussing how vicious and wily is the yetzer hara.

"Yes," said the Chofetz Chaim, "and that yetzer hara also says, 'Bachurim, talk about how bad I am, talk about how evil I am, talk and talk and talk all day... as long it keeps you from learning Torah — then I won.'"

As we prepare to start the new day, having recited the *Birchos HaTorah* and asked that our hearts be open to Hashem's Torah, we ask for Divine help in conquering the *yetzer hara* that will be lying in wait with just one goal: to take us away from the Torah.

וְהַרְחִיקֵנוּ מֵאָדָם רָע וּמֵחָבֵר רָע —
Distance us from an evil person
and from an evil companion.

Sometimes, a person can be good and true, loyal and devoted. He is a good person, but that still doesn't make him a good companion. A good friend calls for more than being a good person.

Rav Mordechai Sharabi would explain that the letters that form the word חָבֵר, *friend* — *ches, veis,* and *reish* — can be rearranged to form the word חֶרֶב, *sword,* and can also be rearranged to form the word בָּרַח, *to escape.* One must flee from a friend who creates a negative influence as if from the sword; but what about one who is a good influence? A wise person attaches himself to good friends, knowing that a good friend opens up the gates to every sort of blessing.

Grant us today and every day grace, kindness, and mercy in Your eyes and in the eyes of all who see us, and bestow beneficent kindnesses upon us. Blessed are You, HASHEM, Who bestows beneficent kindnesses upon His people Israel.

וְתִתְּנֵנוּ הַיּוֹם וּבְכָל יוֹם לְחֵן וּלְחֶסֶד
וּלְרַחֲמִים בְּעֵינֶיךָ וּבְעֵינֵי כָל רוֹאֵינוּ —
*Grant us today and every day grace,
kindness, and mercy in Your eyes
and in the eyes of all who see us.*

The request is for הַיּוֹם וּבְכָל יוֹם, *today and every day*, because at this moment, the dawn of a new day, we realize just what a gift life is. The sun is soaring high in the sky and we feel invigorated and breathe the fresh air in His blessed world, and so we ask not just for the day ahead, but for many additional days as well.

לְחֵן וּלְחֶסֶד וּלְרַחֲמִים בְּעֵינֶיךָ —
Grace, kindness, and mercy in Your eyes.

Every single Yid, writes the Chiddushei HaRim, has a special *nekudah,* a point of *nesias chein,* with which he and only he can elicit favor from the Ribbono Shel Olam. No person can ascertain how and with what he is *nosei chein* by Hashem, but there is something special within each of us that generates love from the Creator specifically to us.

> *Rav Shlomo Freifeld was sitting with the sefer Shaarei Aharon when he suddenly banged on the table, as if he'd discovered something remarkable. His son-in-law wondered what Rav Shlomo had seen that had affected him so profoundly, and Rav Shlomo showed him the words of a Midrash, quoted in the sefer,*

that teach that the middah of kaas, anger, causes a person to lose his natural "nesias chein," ability to elicit favor.

"Every Yid has chein," Rav Shlomo said, "and every talmid who has ever come to this yeshivah was oozing with chein. When a new bachur comes here, I feel an instant connection with him, drawn to try to help him and to develop a relationship with him. Yet there is a certain new bachur who came and, as hard as I try, I cannot find that nekudah of chein in him: it's like it's blocked. It was frustrating me greatly, but then I saw this Midrash and I understand the impediment. The bachur tends to anger easily, and now that I know this, I also know the way to help him. We will work on finding a way to control his anger, and then that natural chein will burst through... that is why I'm excited."

Perhaps this is the flow of the *tefillah*. Help me control my *yetzer hara*, we ask Hashem, and then, our natural charm and appeal will be readily evident.

Someone once asked Rav Aryeh Finkel how a person can ask, in one phrase, to earn favor in the eyes of Hashem and also of humans — aren't they two very different requests? Rav Aryeh quoted the Mishnah: הוּא הָיָה אוֹמֵר, כָּל שֶׁרוּחַ הַבְּרִיּוֹת נוֹחָה הֵימֶנּוּ, רוּחַ הַמָּקוֹם נוֹחָה הֵימֶנּוּ, *If the spirit of one's fellow is pleased with him, the spirit of the Omnipresent is pleased with him (Pirkei Avos 3:11)*. We are asking, Rav Aryeh explained, that we find favor in the eyes of Hakadosh Baruch Hu — how so? By finding favor in the eyes of other people.

וְתִגְמְלֵנוּ חֲסָדִים טוֹבִים —
And bestow beneficent kindnesses upon us.

What is meant by *chassadim tovim* — are there kindnesses that are not beneficent?

Yaakov Avinu, we find, was worried about expending his

merits when he earned miracles. Some commentators explain this *tefillah* as a request for Divine kindness, not by using up our own merits, but rather, through accessing *chassadim* that come from Hashem's benevolence.

The Siach Yitzchak explains that often, a man does a favor for his friend. This is a *chessed*. But a human cannot foresee the results of the kindness he performed. A person can lend money to a friend with which to open a business, but then the business fails. The loan, it turns out, was a *chessed*, but it did not result in *chessed*.

We ask Hashem that the *chassadim* He performs with us should be the sort of *chassadim* that lead to our ultimate good, *chassadim tovim*, every door that opens leading to more *berachah*.

סדר השכמת הבוקר ~§

The Complete Text of the
Early Morning Prayers —
Modeh Ani through the Blessings

As we wake up, we feel deeply grateful to God for having restored our faculties. Before getting out of bed or beginning any conversation or activity, we immediately declare our gratitude and firmly resolve to serve our Creator:

מוֹדֶה אֲנִי לְפָנֶיךָ, מֶלֶךְ חַי וְקַיָּם, שֶׁהֶחֱזַרְתָּ בִּי נִשְׁמָתִי בְּחֶמְלָה — רַבָּה אֱמוּנָתֶךָ.

Wash the hands according to the ritual procedure: pick up the cup of water with the right hand, pass it to the left, and pour water over the right. Then with the right hand pour over the left. Follow this procedure until water has been poured over each hand three times. Then recite:

רֵאשִׁית חָכְמָה יִרְאַת יהוה, שֵׂכֶל טוֹב לְכָל עֹשֵׂיהֶם, תְּהִלָּתוֹ עֹמֶדֶת לָעַד.[1] בָּרוּךְ שֵׁם כְּבוֹד מַלְכוּתוֹ לְעוֹלָם וָעֶד.[2] תּוֹרָה צִוָּה לָנוּ מֹשֶׁה, מוֹרָשָׁה קְהִלַּת יַעֲקֹב.[3] שְׁמַע בְּנִי מוּסַר אָבִיךָ, וְאַל תִּטֹּשׁ תּוֹרַת אִמֶּךָ.[4] תּוֹרָה תְּהֵא אֱמוּנָתִי, וְאֵל שַׁדַּי בְּעֶזְרָתִי. וְאַתֶּם הַדְּבֵקִים בַּיהוה אֱלֹהֵיכֶם, חַיִּים כֻּלְּכֶם הַיּוֹם.[5] לִישׁוּעָתְךָ קִוִּיתִי יהוה.[6]

✦ לְבִישַׁת צִיצִית ✦

Hold the *tallis kattan* in readiness to put on, inspect the *tzitzis* (see commentary), and recite the following blessing. Then, put on the *tallis kattan* and kiss the *tzitzis*. One who wears a *tallis* for *Shacharis* does not recite this blessing (see commentary).

בָּרוּךְ אַתָּה יהוה אֱלֹהֵינוּ מֶלֶךְ הָעוֹלָם, אֲשֶׁר קִדְּשָׁנוּ בְּמִצְוֹתָיו, וְצִוָּנוּ עַל מִצְוַת צִיצִת.

יְהִי רָצוֹן מִלְּפָנֶיךָ, יהוה אֱלֹהַי וֵאלֹהֵי אֲבוֹתַי, שֶׁתְּהֵא חֲשׁוּבָה מִצְוַת צִיצִת לְפָנֶיךָ, כְּאִלּוּ קִיַּמְתִּיהָ בְּכָל פְּרָטֶיהָ וְדִקְדּוּקֶיהָ וְכַוָּנוֹתֶיהָ, וְתַרְיַ"ג מִצְוֹת הַתְּלוּיִים בָּהּ. אָמֵן סֶלָה.

---

(1) *Tehillim* 111:10. (3) *Devarim* 33:4. (4) *Mishlei* 1:8. (5) *Devarim* 4:4. (6) *Bereishis* 49:18.

✌ Upon Arising ✌

As we wake up, we feel deeply grateful to God for having restored our faculties. Before getting out of bed or beginning any conversation or activity, we immediately declare our gratitude and firmly resolve to serve our Creator:

מוֹדֶה אֲנִי *I gratefully thank You, O living and eternal King, for You have returned my soul within me with compassion — abundant is Your faithfulness!*

Wash the hands according to the ritual procedure: pick up the cup of water with the right hand, pass it to the left, and pour water over the right. Then with the right hand pour over the left. Follow this procedure until water has been poured over each hand three times. Then recite:

רֵאשִׁית חָכְמָה *The beginning of wisdom is the fear of HASHEM — good understanding to all who practice them; His praise endures forever.[1] Blessed is the Name of His glorious kingdom for all eternity.[2] The Torah that was commanded to us by Moshe is the heritage of the congregation of Yaakov.[3] Hear, my child, the discipline of your father, and do not forsake the teaching of your mother.[4] The Torah should be my faith, and El Shaddai should assist me. But you who cling to HASHEM, your God — you are all alive today.[5] For Your salvation do I long, O HASHEM![6]*

✌ Putting On Tzitzis ✌

Hold the *tallis kattan* in readiness to put on, inspect the *tzitzis* (see commentary), and recite the following blessing. Then, put on the *tallis kattan* and kiss the *tzitzis*. One who wears a *tallis* for *Shacharis* does not recite this blessing (see commentary).

בָּרוּךְ *Blessed are You, HASHEM, our God, King of the universe, Who has sanctified us with His command-ments, and has commanded us regarding the commandment of tzitzis.*

יְהִי רָצוֹן *May it be Your will, HASHEM, my God and the God of my forefathers, that the commandment of tzitzis be as worthy before You as if I had fulfilled it in all its details, implications, and intentions, as well as the six hundred thirteen commandments that are dependent upon it. Amen, Selah!*

Before putting on the *tallis*, inspect the *tzitzis* (see commentary) while reciting these verses:

בָּרְכִי נַפְשִׁי אֶת יהוה, יהוה אֱלֹהַי גָּדַלְתָּ מְּאֹד, הוֹד וְהָדָר לָבָשְׁתָּ. עֹטֶה אוֹר כַּשַּׂלְמָה, נוֹטֶה שָׁמַיִם כַּיְרִיעָה.[1]

Many recite the following declaration of intent before putting on the *tallis*:

לְשֵׁם יִחוּד קֻדְשָׁא בְּרִיךְ הוּא וּשְׁכִינְתֵּהּ, בִּדְחִילוּ וּרְחִימוּ לְיַחֵד שֵׁם יוּ״ד הֵ״א בְּוָא״ו הֵ״א בְּיִחוּדָא שְׁלִים, בְּשֵׁם כָּל יִשְׂרָאֵל.

הֲרֵינִי מִתְעַטֵּף גּוּפִי בַּצִּיצִת, כֵּן תִּתְעַטֵּף נִשְׁמָתִי וּרְמַ״ח אֵבָרַי וּשְׁסָ״ה גִּידַי בְּאוֹר הַצִּיצִת הָעוֹלֶה תַּרְיַ״ג. וּכְשֵׁם שֶׁאֲנִי מִתְכַּסֶּה בְּטַלִּית בָּעוֹלָם הַזֶּה, כָּךְ אֶזְכֶּה לַחֲלוּקָא דְרַבָּנָן וּלְטַלִּית נָאָה לָעוֹלָם הַבָּא בְּגַן עֵדֶן. וְעַל יְדֵי מִצְוַת צִיצִת תִּנָּצֵל נַפְשִׁי וְרוּחִי וְנִשְׁמָתִי וּתְפִלָּתִי מִן הַחִיצוֹנִים. וְהַטַּלִּית יִפְרֹשׂ כְּנָפָיו עֲלֵיהֶם וְיַצִּילֵם כְּנֶשֶׁר יָעִיר קִנּוֹ, עַל גּוֹזָלָיו יְרַחֵף.[2] וּתְהֵא חֲשׁוּבָה מִצְוַת צִיצִת לִפְנֵי הַקָּדוֹשׁ בָּרוּךְ הוּא כְּאִלוּ קִיַּמְתִּיהָ בְּכָל פְּרָטֶיהָ וְדִקְדּוּקֶיהָ וְכַוָּנוֹתֶיהָ וְתַרְיַ״ג מִצְוֹת הַתְּלוּיִם בָּהּ. אָמֵן סֶלָה.

Unfold the *tallis*, hold it in readiness to wrap around yourself, and recite the following blessing:

בָּרוּךְ אַתָּה יהוה אֱלֹהֵינוּ מֶלֶךְ הָעוֹלָם, אֲשֶׁר קִדְּשָׁנוּ בְּמִצְוֹתָיו, וְצִוָּנוּ לְהִתְעַטֵּף בַּצִּיצִת.

Wrap the *tallis* around your head and body, then recite:

מַה יָּקָר חַסְדְּךָ אֱלֹהִים, וּבְנֵי אָדָם בְּצֵל כְּנָפֶיךָ יֶחֱסָיוּן. יִרְוְיֻן מִדֶּשֶׁן בֵּיתֶךָ, וְנַחַל עֲדָנֶיךָ תַשְׁקֵם. כִּי עִמְּךָ מְקוֹר חַיִּים, בְּאוֹרְךָ נִרְאֶה אוֹר. מְשֹׁךְ חַסְדְּךָ לְיֹדְעֶיךָ, וְצִדְקָתְךָ לְיִשְׁרֵי לֵב.[3]

✑ **Putting On the Tallis** ✑

Before putting on the *tallis,* inspect the *tzitzis* (see commentary) while reciting these verses:

בָּרְכִי נַפְשִׁי **Bless, O my soul, HASHEM; HASHEM, my God, You are very great; You have clothed Yourself in** *majesty and splendor; wrapped in light as with a garment, stretching out the heavens like a curtain.*[1]

Many recite the following declaration of intent before putting on the *tallis:*

לְשֵׁם יִחוּד *For the sake of the unification of the Holy One, Blessed is He, and His Presence, in fear and love to unify the* Name — yud-kei with vav-kei — *in perfect unity, in the name of all Israel.*

הֲרֵינִי *I am ready to wrap my body in tzitzis, so may my soul, my two hundred forty-eight organs, and my three hundred sixty-five sinews be wrapped in the illumination of tzitzis which has the numerical value of six hundred thirteen. Just as I cover myself with a tallis in This World, so may I merit the rabbinical garb and a beautiful cloak in the World to Come in the Garden of Eden. Through the commandment of tzitzis may my life force, spirit, soul, and prayer be rescued from the external forces. May the tallis spread its wings over them and rescue them like an eagle awaking its nest, fluttering over its young.*[2] *May the commandment of tzitzis be worthy before the Holy One, Blessed is He, as if I had fulfilled it in all its details, implications, and intentions, as well as the six hundred thirteen commandments that are dependent upon it. Amen, Selah!*

Unfold the *tallis,* hold it in readiness to wrap around yourself, and recite the following blessing:

בָּרוּךְ *Blessed are You, HASHEM, our God, King of the universe, Who has sanctified us with His command-ments and has commanded us to wrap ourselves in tzitzis.*

Wrap the *tallis* around your head and body, then recite:

מַה יָּקָר *How precious is Your kindness, O God! The sons of man take refuge in the shadow of Your wings. May they be sated from the abundance of Your house; and may You give them to drink from the stream of Your delights. For with You is the source of life — by Your light we shall see light. Extend Your kindness to those who know You, and Your charity to the upright of heart.*[3]

---

(1) *Tehillim* 104:1-2. (2) *Devarim* 32:11. (3) *Tehillim* 36:8-11.

Many recite the following declaration of intent before putting on the *tefillin*:

לְשֵׁם יְחוּד קֻדְשָׁא בְּרִיךְ הוּא וּשְׁכִינְתֵּהּ, בִּדְחִילוּ וּרְחִימוּ
לְיַחֵד שֵׁם יוֹ״ד הֵ״א בְּוָא״ו הֵ״א בְּיִחוּדָא שְׁלִים,
בְּשֵׁם כָּל יִשְׂרָאֵל.

הִנְנִי מְכַוֵּן בַּהֲנָחַת תְּפִילִּין לְקַיֵּם מִצְוַת בּוֹרְאִי, שֶׁצִּוָּנוּ
לְהָנִיחַ תְּפִילִּין, כַּכָּתוּב בְּתוֹרָתוֹ: וּקְשַׁרְתָּם
לְאוֹת עַל יָדֶךָ, וְהָיוּ לְטֹטָפֹת בֵּין עֵינֶיךָ.[1] וְהֵם אַרְבַּע פָּרְשִׁיּוֹת
אֵלּוּ — שְׁמַע, וְהָיָה אִם שָׁמֹעַ, קַדֶּשׁ, וְהָיָה כִּי יְבִאֲךָ —
שֶׁיֵּשׁ בָּהֶם יִחוּדוֹ וְאַחְדוּתוֹ יִתְבָּרַךְ שְׁמוֹ בָּעוֹלָם; וְשֶׁנִּזְכּוֹר
נִסִּים וְנִפְלָאוֹת שֶׁעָשָׂה עִמָּנוּ בְּהוֹצִיאָנוּ מִמִּצְרָיִם; וַאֲשֶׁר
לוֹ הַכֹּחַ וְהַמֶּמְשָׁלָה בָּעֶלְיוֹנִים וּבַתַּחְתּוֹנִים לַעֲשׂוֹת בָּהֶם
כִּרְצוֹנוֹ. וְצִוָּנוּ לְהָנִיחַ עַל הַיָּד, לְזִכְרוֹן זְרוֹעַ הַנְּטוּיָה, וְשֶׁהִיא
נֶגֶד הַלֵּב, לְשַׁעְבֵּד בָּזֶה תַּאֲוַת וּמַחְשְׁבוֹת לִבֵּנוּ לַעֲבוֹדָתוֹ,
יִתְבָּרַךְ שְׁמוֹ. וְעַל הָרֹאשׁ נֶגֶד הַמֹּחַ, שֶׁהַנְּשָׁמָה שֶׁבְּמֹחִי,
עִם שְׁאָר חוּשַׁי וְכֹחוֹתַי, כֻּלָּם יִהְיוּ מְשֻׁעְבָּדִים לַעֲבוֹדָתוֹ,
יִתְבָּרַךְ שְׁמוֹ. וּמִשֶּׁפַע מִצְוַת תְּפִילִּין יִתְמַשֵּׁךְ עָלַי לִהְיוֹת
לִי חַיִּים אֲרוּכִים, וְשֶׁפַע קֹדֶשׁ, וּמַחְשָׁבוֹת קְדוֹשׁוֹת בְּלִי
הִרְהוּר חֵטְא וְעָוֹן כְּלָל; וְשֶׁלֹּא יְפַתֵּנוּ וְלֹא יִתְגָּרֶה בָּנוּ יֵצֶר
הָרָע, וְיַנִּיחֵנוּ לַעֲבֹד אֶת יהוה כַּאֲשֶׁר עִם לְבָבֵנוּ. וִיהִי רָצוֹן
מִלְּפָנֶיךָ, יהוה אֱלֹהֵינוּ וֵאלֹהֵי אֲבוֹתֵינוּ, שֶׁתְּהֵא חֲשׁוּבָה
מִצְוַת הֲנָחַת תְּפִילִּין לִפְנֵי הַקָּדוֹשׁ בָּרוּךְ הוּא, כְּאִלּוּ קִיַּמְתִּיהָ
בְּכָל פְּרָטֶיהָ וְדִקְדּוּקֶיהָ וְכַוָּנוֹתֶיהָ, וְתַרְיַ״ג מִצְוֹת הַתְּלוּיִם בָּהּ.
אָמֵן סֶלָה.

Stand while putting on *tefillin*. Place the arm-*tefillin* upon the left biceps (or the right biceps of one who writes left-handed), hold it in place ready for tightening, then recite the following blessing:

בָּרוּךְ אַתָּה יהוה אֱלֹהֵינוּ מֶלֶךְ הָעוֹלָם, אֲשֶׁר קִדְּשָׁנוּ
בְּמִצְוֹתָיו, וְצִוָּנוּ לְהָנִיחַ תְּפִילִּין.

⸂ Order of Putting On Tefillin ⸃

Many recite the following declaration of intent before putting on the *tefillin*:

לְשֵׁם For the sake of the unification of the Holy One, Blessed is He, and His Presence, in fear and love to unify the Name — *yud-kei with vav-kei* — in perfect unity, in the name of all Israel.

הִנְנִי מְכַוֵּן Behold, in putting on tefillin I intend to fulfill the commandment of my Creator, Who has commanded us to put on tefillin, as is written in His Torah: "Bind them as a sign upon your arm and let them be tefillin between your eyes."[1] These four portions [contained in the tefillin] — [1] "Shema" (Devarim 6:4-9); [2] "And it will come to pass, if you will listen" (ibid. 11:13-21); [3] "Sanctify" (Shemos 13:1-10); and [4] "And it will come to pass when He shall bring you" (ibid. 13:11-16) — contain His Oneness and Unity, may His Name be blessed, in the universe; so that we will remember the miracles and wonders that He did with us when He took us from Egypt; and that He has the strength and dominion over those above and those below to do with them as He wishes. He has commanded us to put [tefillin] upon the arm to recall the "outstretched arm" [of the Exodus] and that it be opposite the heart so that it will subjugate the desires and thoughts of our heart to His service, may His Name be blessed; and upon the head opposite the brain, so that the soul that is in my brain, together with my other senses and potentials, may all be subjugated to His service, may His Name be blessed. May some of the spiritual influence of the commandment of tefillin be extended upon me so that I have a long life, a flow of holiness, and holy thoughts, without even an inkling of sin or iniquity; and that the evil inclination will not seduce us nor incite against us, and that it permit us to serve HASHEM as is our hearts' desire. May it be Your will, HASHEM, our God and the God of our forefathers, that the commandment of putting on tefillin be considered as worthy before the Holy One, Blessed is He, as if I had fulfilled it in all its details, implications, and intentions, as well as the six hundred thirteen commandments that are dependent upon it. Amen, Selah.

Stand while putting on *tefillin*. Place the arm-*tefillin* upon the left biceps (or the right biceps of one who writes left-handed), hold it in place ready for tightening, then recite the following blessing:

בָּרוּךְ Blessed are You, HASHEM, our God, King of the universe, Who has sanctified us with His command-ments and has commanded us to put on tefillin.

---

(1) *Devarim* 6:8.

Tighten the arm-*tefillin* and wrap the strap seven times around the arm. Without any interruption whatsoever, put the head-*tefillin* in place, above the hairline and opposite the space between the eyes. Before tightening the head-*tefillin* recite the following blessing:

בָּרוּךְ אַתָּה יהוה אֱלֹהֵינוּ מֶלֶךְ הָעוֹלָם, אֲשֶׁר קִדְּשָׁנוּ בְּמִצְוֹתָיו, וְצִוָּנוּ עַל מִצְוַת תְּפִלִּין.

Tighten the head-*tefillin* and recite:

בָּרוּךְ שֵׁם כְּבוֹד מַלְכוּתוֹ לְעוֹלָם וָעֶד.

After the head-*tefillin* is securely in place, recite:

וּמֵחָכְמָתְךָ אֵל עֶלְיוֹן, תַּאֲצִיל עָלַי; וּמִבִּינָתְךָ תְּבִינֵנִי; וּבְחַסְדְּךָ תַּגְדִּיל עָלַי; וּבִגְבוּרָתְךָ תַּצְמִית אוֹיְבַי וְקָמַי. וְשֶׁמֶן הַטּוֹב תָּרִיק עַל שִׁבְעָה קְנֵי הַמְּנוֹרָה, לְהַשְׁפִּיעַ טוּבְךָ לִבְרִיּוֹתֶיךָ. פּוֹתֵחַ אֶת יָדֶךָ, וּמַשְׂבִּיעַ לְכָל חַי רָצוֹן.[1]

Wrap the strap around the middle finger and hand according to your custom. While doing this, recite:

וְאֵרַשְׂתִּיךְ לִי לְעוֹלָם, וְאֵרַשְׂתִּיךְ לִי בְּצֶדֶק וּבְמִשְׁפָּט וּבְחֶסֶד וּבְרַחֲמִים. וְאֵרַשְׂתִּיךְ לִי בֶּאֱמוּנָה, וְיָדַעַתְּ אֶת יהוה.[2]

It is proper, while wearing *tefillin*, to recite the four Scriptural passages that are contained in the *tefillin*. Two of them — שְׁמַע and וְהָיָה אִם שָׁמֹעַ — will be recited later as part of *Krias Shema*. The other two passages, given below, are recited either after putting on the *tefillin* or before removing them.

שמות יג:א-י

וַיְדַבֵּר יהוה אֶל מֹשֶׁה לֵּאמֹר: קַדֶּשׁ לִי כָל בְּכוֹר, פֶּטֶר כָּל רֶחֶם בִּבְנֵי יִשְׂרָאֵל בָּאָדָם וּבַבְּהֵמָה, לִי הוּא. וַיֹּאמֶר מֹשֶׁה אֶל הָעָם: זָכוֹר אֶת הַיּוֹם הַזֶּה אֲשֶׁר יְצָאתֶם מִמִּצְרַיִם מִבֵּית עֲבָדִים, כִּי בְּחֹזֶק יָד הוֹצִיא יהוה אֶתְכֶם מִזֶּה, וְלֹא יֵאָכֵל חָמֵץ. הַיּוֹם אַתֶּם יֹצְאִים, בְּחֹדֶשׁ

Tighten the arm-*tefillin* and wrap the strap seven times around the arm. Without any interruption whatsoever, put the head-*tefillin* in place, above the hairline and opposite the space between the eyes. Before tightening the head-*tefillin* recite the following blessing:

בָּרוּךְ **Blessed** *are You, HASHEM, our God, King of the universe, Who has sanctified us with His command-ments and has commanded us regarding the commandment of tefillin.*

Tighten the head-*tefillin* and recite:

Blessed is the Name of His glorious kingdom for all eternity.

After the head-*tefillin* is securely in place, recite:

וּמֵחָכְמָתְךָ **From** *Your wisdom, O supreme God, may You imbue me; from Your understanding give me understanding; with Your kindness do greatly with me; with Your power cut down my foes and rebels. [May] You pour goodly oil upon the seven arms of the menorah, to cause Your good to flow to Your creatures. [May] You open Your hand and satisfy the desire of every living thing.*[1]

Wrap the strap around the middle finger and hand according to your custom. While doing this, recite:

וְאֵרַשְׂתִּיךְ *I will betroth you to Me forever, and I will betroth you to Me with righteousness, justice, kindness, and mercy. I will betroth you to Me with faithfulness, and you shall know HASHEM.*[2]

It is proper, while wearing *tefillin*, to recite the four Scriptural passages that are contained in the *tefillin*. Two of them — שְׁמַע, *"Shema,"* and וְהָיָה אִם שָׁמֹעַ, *"It will come to pass, if you will listen"* — will be recited later as part of *Krias Shema*. The other two passages, given below, are recited either after putting on the *tefillin* or before removing them.

Exodus 13:1-10

וַיְדַבֵּר *HASHEM spoke to Moshe, saying: Sanctify to Me every firstborn, the first issue of every womb among the Children of Israel, both of man and of beast, is Mine. Moshe said to the people: Remember this day on which you departed from Egypt, from the house of bondage, for with a strong hand HASHEM took you from here, and therefore no chametz may be eaten. Today you are leaving in the month of*

---

(1) *Tehillim* 145:16. (2) *Hoshea* 2:21-22.

הָאָבִיב. וְהָיָה כִי יְבִיאֲךָ יהוה אֶל אֶרֶץ הַכְּנַעֲנִי וְהַחִתִּי
וְהָאֱמֹרִי וְהַחִוִּי וְהַיְבוּסִי אֲשֶׁר נִשְׁבַּע לַאֲבֹתֶיךָ לָתֶת
לָךְ, אֶרֶץ זָבַת חָלָב וּדְבָשׁ, וְעָבַדְתָּ אֶת הָעֲבֹדָה הַזֹּאת
בַּחֹדֶשׁ הַזֶּה. שִׁבְעַת יָמִים תֹּאכַל מַצֹּת, וּבַיּוֹם הַשְּׁבִיעִי
חַג לַיהוה. מַצּוֹת יֵאָכֵל אֵת שִׁבְעַת הַיָּמִים, וְלֹא יֵרָאֶה
לְךָ חָמֵץ, וְלֹא יֵרָאֶה לְךָ שְׂאֹר, בְּכָל גְּבֻלֶךָ. וְהִגַּדְתָּ
לְבִנְךָ בַּיּוֹם הַהוּא לֵאמֹר: בַּעֲבוּר זֶה עָשָׂה יהוה לִי
בְּצֵאתִי מִמִּצְרָיִם. וְהָיָה לְךָ לְאוֹת עַל יָדְךָ, וּלְזִכָּרוֹן
בֵּין עֵינֶיךָ, לְמַעַן תִּהְיֶה תּוֹרַת יהוה בְּפִיךָ, כִּי בְּיָד
חֲזָקָה הוֹצִאֲךָ יהוה מִמִּצְרָיִם. וְשָׁמַרְתָּ אֶת הַחֻקָּה
הַזֹּאת לְמוֹעֲדָהּ, מִיָּמִים יָמִימָה.

שמות יג:יא-טז

וְהָיָה כִּי יְבִאֲךָ יהוה אֶל אֶרֶץ הַכְּנַעֲנִי, כַּאֲשֶׁר
נִשְׁבַּע לְךָ וְלַאֲבֹתֶיךָ, וּנְתָנָהּ לָךְ. וְהַעֲבַרְתָּ כָל
פֶּטֶר רֶחֶם לַיהוה, וְכָל פֶּטֶר שֶׁגֶר בְּהֵמָה אֲשֶׁר יִהְיֶה
לְךָ, הַזְּכָרִים לַיהוה. וְכָל פֶּטֶר חֲמֹר תִּפְדֶּה בְשֶׂה, וְאִם
לֹא תִפְדֶּה וַעֲרַפְתּוֹ, וְכֹל בְּכוֹר אָדָם בְּבָנֶיךָ תִּפְדֶּה.
וְהָיָה כִּי יִשְׁאָלְךָ בִנְךָ מָחָר לֵאמֹר: מַה זֹּאת, וְאָמַרְתָּ
אֵלָיו: בְּחֹזֶק יָד הוֹצִיאָנוּ יהוה מִמִּצְרַיִם מִבֵּית עֲבָדִים.
וַיְהִי כִּי הִקְשָׁה פַרְעֹה לְשַׁלְּחֵנוּ, וַיַּהֲרֹג יהוה כָּל בְּכוֹר
בְּאֶרֶץ מִצְרַיִם, מִבְּכֹר אָדָם וְעַד בְּכוֹר בְּהֵמָה, עַל כֵּן
אֲנִי זֹבֵחַ לַיהוה כָּל פֶּטֶר רֶחֶם הַזְּכָרִים, וְכָל בְּכוֹר בָּנַי
אֶפְדֶּה. וְהָיָה לְאוֹת עַל יָדְכָה, וּלְטוֹטָפֹת בֵּין עֵינֶיךָ, כִּי
בְּחֹזֶק יָד הוֹצִיאָנוּ יהוה מִמִּצְרָיִם.

springtime. And it will come to pass, when HASHEM shall bring you to the land of the Canaanites, Hittites, Emorites, Hivvites, and Jebusites, which He swore to your forefathers to give you — a land flowing with milk and honey — you shall perform this service in this month. Seven days you shall eat matzos, and on the seventh day there shall be a festival to HASHEM. Matzos shall be eaten throughout the seven days; no chametz may be seen in your possession, nor may leaven be seen in your possession in all your borders. And you shall tell your son on that day, saying: "It is because of this that HASHEM acted on my behalf when I left Egypt." And it shall serve you as a sign on your arm and as a reminder between your eyes — so that HASHEM's Torah may be in your mouth; for with a strong hand HASHEM took you from Egypt. And you shall observe this ordinance at its designated time from year to year.

Exodus 13:11-16

וְהָיָה And it shall come to pass, when HASHEM will bring you to the land of the Canaanites as He swore to you and your forefathers, and will have given it to you. Then you shall set apart every first issue of the womb to HASHEM, and every first issue that is dropped by cattle that belong to you, the males shall belong to HASHEM. Every first issue of a donkey you shall redeem with a lamb or kid; if you do not redeem it, then you must axe the back of its neck. And you must redeem every human firstborn among your sons. And it shall be when your son asks you at some future time, "What is this?" you shall answer him, "With a strong hand HASHEM took us from Egypt, from the house of bondage. And it happened, when Pharaoh stubbornly refused to let us go, that HASHEM killed all the firstborn in the land of Egypt, from the firstborn of man to the firstborn of beast. Therefore, I sacrifice to HASHEM all first male issue of the womb, and redeem all the firstborn of my sons. And it shall be a sign upon your arm and totafos between your eyes, for with a strong hand HASHEM took us from Egypt."

Recite the following collection of verses upon entering the synagogue:

מַה טֹּבוּ אֹהָלֶיךָ יַעֲקֹב, מִשְׁכְּנֹתֶיךָ יִשְׂרָאֵל.¹ וַאֲנִי בְּרֹב חַסְדְּךָ אָבוֹא בֵיתֶךָ, אֶשְׁתַּחֲוֶה אֶל הֵיכַל קָדְשְׁךָ בְּיִרְאָתֶךָ.² יהוה אָהַבְתִּי מְעוֹן בֵּיתֶךָ, וּמְקוֹם מִשְׁכַּן כְּבוֹדֶךָ.³ וַאֲנִי אֶשְׁתַּחֲוֶה וְאֶכְרָעָה, אֶבְרְכָה לִפְנֵי יהוה עֹשִׂי.⁴ וַאֲנִי, תְפִלָּתִי לְךָ יהוה עֵת רָצוֹן, אֱלֹהִים בְּרָב חַסְדֶּךָ, עֲנֵנִי בֶּאֱמֶת יִשְׁעֶךָ.⁵

אֲדוֹן עוֹלָם אֲשֶׁר מָלַךְ בְּטֶרֶם כָּל יְצִיר נִבְרָא. לְעֵת נַעֲשָׂה בְחֶפְצוֹ כֹּל, אֲזַי מֶלֶךְ שְׁמוֹ נִקְרָא. וְאַחֲרֵי כִּכְלוֹת הַכֹּל, לְבַדּוֹ יִמְלוֹךְ נוֹרָא. וְהוּא הָיָה וְהוּא הֹוֶה, וְהוּא יִהְיֶה בְּתִפְאָרָה. וְהוּא אֶחָד וְאֵין שֵׁנִי לְהַמְשִׁיל לוֹ לְהַחְבִּירָה. בְּלִי רֵאשִׁית בְּלִי תַכְלִית, וְלוֹ הָעֹז וְהַמִּשְׂרָה. וְהוּא אֵלִי וְחַי גֹּאֲלִי, וְצוּר חֶבְלִי בְּעֵת צָרָה. וְהוּא נִסִּי וּמָנוֹס לִי, מְנָת כּוֹסִי בְּיוֹם אֶקְרָא. בְּיָדוֹ אַפְקִיד רוּחִי בְּעֵת אִישַׁן וְאָעִירָה. וְעִם רוּחִי גְּוִיָּתִי, יהוה לִי וְלֹא אִירָא.

יִגְדַּל אֱלֹהִים חַי וְיִשְׁתַּבַּח, נִמְצָא וְאֵין עֵת אֶל מְצִיאוּתוֹ. אֶחָד וְאֵין יָחִיד כְּיִחוּדוֹ, נֶעְלָם וְגַם אֵין סוֹף לְאַחְדּוּתוֹ. אֵין לוֹ דְמוּת הַגּוּף וְאֵינוֹ גוּף, לֹא נַעֲרוֹךְ אֵלָיו קְדֻשָּׁתוֹ. קַדְמוֹן לְכָל דָּבָר אֲשֶׁר נִבְרָא, רִאשׁוֹן וְאֵין רֵאשִׁית לְרֵאשִׁיתוֹ. הִנּוֹ אֲדוֹן עוֹלָם לְכָל נוֹצָר, יוֹרֶה גְדֻלָּתוֹ וּמַלְכוּתוֹ. שֶׁפַע נְבוּאָתוֹ נְתָנוֹ, אֶל אַנְשֵׁי סְגֻלָּתוֹ וְתִפְאַרְתּוֹ. לֹא קָם בְּיִשְׂרָאֵל כְּמֹשֶׁה עוֹד, נָבִיא וּמַבִּיט אֶת תְּמוּנָתוֹ. תּוֹרַת אֱמֶת נָתַן לְעַמּוֹ אֵל,

↪ **Morning Blessings** ↩

Recite the following collection of verses upon entering the synagogue:

מַה טֹּבוּ How goodly are your tents, O Yaakov, your dwelling places, O Yisrael.[1] As for me, through Your abundant kindness I will enter Your House; I will prostrate myself toward Your Holy Sanctuary in awe of You.[2] O HASHEM, I love the House where You dwell, and the place where Your glory resides.[3] I shall prostrate myself and bow, I shall kneel before HASHEM my Maker.[4] As for me, may my prayer to You, HASHEM, be at a favorable time; O God, in Your abundant kindness, answer me with the truth of Your salvation.[5]

עוֹלָם Master of the universe, Who reigned before any form was created, At the time when His will brought all into being — then as "King" was His Name proclaimed. After all has ceased to be, He, the Awesome One, will reign alone. It is He Who was, He Who is, and He Who shall remain, in splendor. He is One — there is no second to compare to Him, to declare as His equal. Without beginning, without conclusion — His is the power and dominion. He is my God, my living Redeemer, Rock of my pain in time of distress. He is my banner, a refuge for me, the portion in my cup on the day I call. Into His hand I shall entrust my spirit when I go to sleep — and I shall awaken! With my spirit shall my body remain. HASHEM is with me, I shall not fear.

יִגְדַּל Exalted be the Living God and praised, He exists — unbounded by time is His existence. He is One — and there is no unity like His Oneness. Inscrutable and infinite is His Oneness. He has no semblance of a body nor has He a body; and nothing compares to His holiness. He preceded every being that was created — the First, and nothing precedes His precedence. Behold! He is Master of the universe to every creature, He demonstrates His greatness and His sovereignty. He granted His flow of prophecy to His treasured, splendrous people. In Israel none like Moshe arose again — a prophet who perceived His vision clearly. God gave His people a Torah of truth,

_____

(1) *Bamidbar* 24:5. (2) *Tehillim* 5:8. (3) 26:8. (4) Cf. 95:6. (5) 69:14.

עַל יַד נְבִיאוֹ נֶאֱמַן בֵּיתוֹ. לֹא יַחֲלִיף הָאֵל וְלֹא יָמִיר דָּתוֹ, לְעוֹלָמִים לְזוּלָתוֹ. צוֹפֶה וְיוֹדֵעַ סְתָרֵינוּ, מַבִּיט לְסוֹף דָּבָר בְּקַדְמָתוֹ. גּוֹמֵל לְאִישׁ חֶסֶד כְּמִפְעָלוֹ, נוֹתֵן לְרָשָׁע רָע כְּרִשְׁעָתוֹ. יִשְׁלַח לְקֵץ הַיָּמִין מְשִׁיחֵנוּ, לִפְדּוֹת מְחַכֵּי קֵץ יְשׁוּעָתוֹ. מֵתִים יְחַיֶּה אֵל בְּרֹב חַסְדּוֹ, בָּרוּךְ עֲדֵי עַד שֵׁם תְּהִלָּתוֹ.

Although many hold that the blessing עַל נְטִילַת יָדַיִם should be recited immediately after the ritual washing of the hands upon arising, others customarily recite it at this point. Similarly, some recite אֲשֶׁר יָצַר immediately after relieving themselves in the morning, while others recite it here.

בָּרוּךְ אַתָּה יהוה אֱלֹהֵינוּ מֶלֶךְ הָעוֹלָם, אֲשֶׁר קִדְּשָׁנוּ בְּמִצְוֹתָיו, וְצִוָּנוּ עַל נְטִילַת יָדָיִם.

בָּרוּךְ אַתָּה יהוה אֱלֹהֵינוּ מֶלֶךְ הָעוֹלָם, אֲשֶׁר יָצַר אֶת הָאָדָם בְּחָכְמָה, וּבָרָא בוֹ נְקָבִים נְקָבִים, חֲלוּלִים חֲלוּלִים. גָּלוּי וְיָדוּעַ לִפְנֵי כִסֵּא כְבוֹדֶךָ, שֶׁאִם יִפָּתֵחַ אֶחָד מֵהֶם, אוֹ יִסָּתֵם אֶחָד מֵהֶם, אִי אֶפְשָׁר לְהִתְקַיֵּם וְלַעֲמוֹד לְפָנֶיךָ (אֲפִילוּ שָׁעָה אֶחָת). בָּרוּךְ אַתָּה יהוה, רוֹפֵא כָל בָּשָׂר וּמַפְלִיא לַעֲשׂוֹת.

At this point, some recite אֱלֹהַי נְשָׁמָה (p. 144).

⤨ בִּרְכוֹת הַתּוֹרָה ⤧

It is forbidden to study or recite Torah passages before reciting the following blessings. However, these blessings need not be repeated if one studies at various times of the day. Although many *siddurim* begin a new paragraph at וְהַעֲרֶב נָא, according to the vast majority of commentators the first blessing continues until לְעַמּוֹ יִשְׂרָאֵל.

בָּרוּךְ אַתָּה יהוה אֱלֹהֵינוּ מֶלֶךְ הָעוֹלָם, אֲשֶׁר קִדְּשָׁנוּ בְּמִצְוֹתָיו, וְצִוָּנוּ לַעֲסוֹק בְּדִבְרֵי תוֹרָה. וְהַעֲרֶב נָא יהוה אֱלֹהֵינוּ אֶת דִּבְרֵי תוֹרָתְךָ בְּפִינוּ וּבְפִי עַמְּךָ בֵּית יִשְׂרָאֵל. וְנִהְיֶה אֲנַחְנוּ וְצֶאֱצָאֵינוּ [וְצֶאֱצָאֵי

by means of His prophet, the most trusted of His household. God will never amend nor exchange His law for any other one, for all eternity. He scrutinizes and knows our hidden-most secrets; He perceives a matter's outcome from its start. He recompenses man with kindness according to his deed; He assigns evil to the wicked according to his wickedness. By the End of Days He will send our Mashiach, to redeem those longing for His final salvation. God will revive the dead in His abundant kindness — Blessed forever is His praised Name.

Although many hold that the blessing עַל נְטִילַת יָדַיִם should be recited immediately after the ritual washing of the hands upon arising, others customarily recite it at this point. Similarly, some recite אֲשֶׁר יָצַר immediately after relieving themselves in the morning, while others recite it here.

בָּרוּךְ Blessed are You, HASHEM, our God, King of the universe, Who has sanctified us with His command-ments and has commanded us regarding washing the hands.

בָּרוּךְ Blessed are You, HASHEM, our God, King of the universe, Who fashioned man with wisdom and created within him many openings and many cavities. It is obvious and known before Your Throne of Glory that if but one of them were to be ruptured or but one of them were to be blocked, it would be impossible to survive and to stand before You (for even one hour). Blessed are You, HASHEM, Who heals all flesh and acts wondrously.

At this point, some recite אֱלֹהַי נְשָׁמָה, "My God, the soul . . ." (p. 144).

✺ Blessings of the Torah ✺

It is forbidden to study or recite Torah passages before reciting the following blessings. However, these blessings need not be repeated if one studies at various times of the day. Although many siddurim begin a new paragraph at וְהַעֲרֶב נָא, "Please . . . sweeten," according to the vast majority of commentators the first blessing continues until לְעַמּוֹ יִשְׂרָאֵל, ". . . to His people Israel."

בָּרוּךְ Blessed are You, HASHEM, our God, King of the universe, Who has sanctified us with His commandments and has commanded us to engross ourselves in the words of Torah. Sweeten, please, HASHEM, our God, the words of Your Torah in our mouth and in the mouth of Your people, the House of Israel. May we and our offspring [and the offsprings

צֶאֱצָאֵינוּ] וְצֶאֱצָאֵי עַמְּךָ בֵּית יִשְׂרָאֵל, כֻּלָּנוּ יוֹדְעֵי שְׁמֶךָ וְלוֹמְדֵי תוֹרָתֶךָ לִשְׁמָהּ. בָּרוּךְ אַתָּה יְהֹוָה, הַמְלַמֵּד תּוֹרָה לְעַמּוֹ יִשְׂרָאֵל.

בָּרוּךְ אַתָּה יְהֹוָה אֱלֹהֵינוּ מֶלֶךְ הָעוֹלָם, אֲשֶׁר בָּחַר בָּנוּ מִכָּל הָעַמִּים וְנָתַן לָנוּ אֶת תּוֹרָתוֹ. בָּרוּךְ אַתָּה יְהֹוָה, נוֹתֵן הַתּוֹרָה.

במדבר ו:כד-כו

יְבָרֶכְךָ יְהֹוָה וְיִשְׁמְרֶךָ. יָאֵר יְהֹוָה פָּנָיו אֵלֶיךָ וִיחֻנֶּךָּ. יִשָּׂא יְהֹוָה פָּנָיו אֵלֶיךָ, וְיָשֵׂם לְךָ שָׁלוֹם.

משנה, פאה א:א

אֵלּוּ דְבָרִים שֶׁאֵין לָהֶם שִׁעוּר: הַפֵּאָה וְהַבִּכּוּרִים וְהָרַאְיוֹן וּגְמִילוּת חֲסָדִים וְתַלְמוּד תּוֹרָה.

שבת קכז

אֵלּוּ דְבָרִים שֶׁאָדָם אוֹכֵל פֵּרוֹתֵיהֶם בָּעוֹלָם הַזֶּה וְהַקֶּרֶן קַיֶּמֶת לוֹ לָעוֹלָם הַבָּא. וְאֵלּוּ הֵן: כִּבּוּד אָב וָאֵם, וּגְמִילוּת חֲסָדִים, וְהַשְׁכָּמַת בֵּית הַמִּדְרָשׁ שַׁחֲרִית וְעַרְבִית, וְהַכְנָסַת אוֹרְחִים, וּבִקּוּר חוֹלִים, וְהַכְנָסַת כַּלָּה, וּלְוָיַת הַמֵּת, וְעִיּוּן תְּפִלָּה, וַהֲבָאַת שָׁלוֹם בֵּין אָדָם לַחֲבֵרוֹ — וְתַלְמוּד תּוֹרָה כְּנֶגֶד כֻּלָּם.

אֱלֹהַי, נְשָׁמָה שֶׁנָּתַתָּ בִּי טְהוֹרָה הִיא. אַתָּה בְרָאתָהּ אַתָּה יְצַרְתָּהּ, אַתָּה נְפַחְתָּהּ בִּי, וְאַתָּה מְשַׁמְּרָהּ בְּקִרְבִּי, וְאַתָּה עָתִיד לִטְּלָהּ מִמֶּנִּי, וּלְהַחֲזִירָהּ בִּי לֶעָתִיד לָבֹא. כָּל זְמַן שֶׁהַנְּשָׁמָה בְקִרְבִּי, מוֹדֶה אֲנִי לְפָנֶיךָ, יְהֹוָה אֱלֹהַי וֵאלֹהֵי אֲבוֹתַי, רִבּוֹן כָּל הַמַּעֲשִׂים, אֲדוֹן כָּל הַנְּשָׁמוֹת. בָּרוּךְ אַתָּה יְהֹוָה, הַמַּחֲזִיר נְשָׁמוֹת לִפְגָרִים מֵתִים.

of our offsprings] and the offspring of Your people, the House of Israel — all of us — know Your Name and study Your Torah for its own sake. Blessed are You, HASHEM, Who teaches Torah to His people Israel.

בָּרוּךְ Blessed are You, HASHEM, our God, King of the universe, Who selected us from all the nations and gave us His Torah. Blessed are You, HASHEM, Giver of the Torah.

Bamidbar 6:24-26

יְבָרֶכְךָ May HASHEM bless you and safeguard you. May HASHEM illuminate His countenance for you and be gracious to you. May HASHEM turn His countenance to you and establish peace for you.

Mishnah, Pe'ah 1:1

אֵלּוּ דְבָרִים These are the precepts that have no prescribed measure: the corner of a field [which must be left for the poor], the first-fruit offering, the pilgrimage, acts of kindness, and Torah study.

Talmud, Shabbos 127a

אֵלּוּ דְבָרִים These are the precepts whose fruits a person enjoys in This World but whose principal remains intact for him in the World to Come. They are: the honor due to father and mother, acts of kindness, early attendance at the house of study morning and evening, hospitality to guests, visiting the sick, providing for a bride, escorting the dead, absorption in prayer, bringing peace between man and his fellow — and the study of Torah is equivalent to them all.

אֱלֹהַי My God, the soul You placed within me is pure. You created it, You fashioned it, You breathed it into me, You safeguard it within me, and eventually You will take it from me, and restore it to me in Time to Come. As long as the soul is within me, I gratefully thank You, HASHEM, my God and the God of my forefathers, Master of all works, Lord of all souls. Blessed are You, HASHEM, Who restores souls to dead bodies.

The *chazzan* recites the following blessings aloud, and the congregation responds אָמֵן to each blessing. Nevertheless, each person must recite these blessings for himself. Some people recite the blessings aloud for one another so that each one can have the merit of responding אָמֵן many times.

בָּרוּךְ אַתָּה יהוה אֱלֹהֵינוּ מֶלֶךְ הָעוֹלָם, אֲשֶׁר נָתַן לַשֶּׂכְוִי בִינָה[1] לְהַבְחִין בֵּין יוֹם וּבֵין לָיְלָה.

בָּרוּךְ אַתָּה יהוה אֱלֹהֵינוּ מֶלֶךְ הָעוֹלָם, שֶׁלֹּא עָשַׂנִי גּוֹי.

בָּרוּךְ אַתָּה יהוה אֱלֹהֵינוּ מֶלֶךְ הָעוֹלָם, שֶׁלֹּא עָשַׂנִי עָבֶד.

Women say:	Men say:
בָּרוּךְ אַתָּה יהוה אֱלֹהֵינוּ מֶלֶךְ הָעוֹלָם, שֶׁעָשַׂנִי כִּרְצוֹנוֹ.	**בָּרוּךְ** אַתָּה יהוה אֱלֹהֵינוּ מֶלֶךְ הָעוֹלָם, שֶׁלֹּא עָשַׂנִי אִשָּׁה.

בָּרוּךְ אַתָּה יהוה אֱלֹהֵינוּ מֶלֶךְ הָעוֹלָם, פּוֹקֵחַ עִוְרִים.[2]

בָּרוּךְ אַתָּה יהוה אֱלֹהֵינוּ מֶלֶךְ הָעוֹלָם, מַלְבִּישׁ עֲרֻמִּים.

בָּרוּךְ אַתָּה יהוה אֱלֹהֵינוּ מֶלֶךְ הָעוֹלָם, מַתִּיר אֲסוּרִים.[3]

בָּרוּךְ אַתָּה יהוה אֱלֹהֵינוּ מֶלֶךְ הָעוֹלָם, זוֹקֵף כְּפוּפִים.[2]

בָּרוּךְ אַתָּה יהוה אֱלֹהֵינוּ מֶלֶךְ הָעוֹלָם, רוֹקַע הָאָרֶץ עַל הַמָּיִם.[4]

Nusach Sefard reverses the order of the following two blessings.

בָּרוּךְ אַתָּה יהוה אֱלֹהֵינוּ מֶלֶךְ הָעוֹלָם, שֶׁעָשָׂה לִי כָּל צָרְכִּי.

בָּרוּךְ אַתָּה יהוה אֱלֹהֵינוּ מֶלֶךְ הָעוֹלָם, הַמֵּכִין מִצְעֲדֵי גָבֶר.[5]

The *chazzan* recites the following blessings aloud, and the congregation responds אָמֵן to each blessing. Nevertheless, each person must recite these blessings for himself. Some people recite the blessings aloud for one another so that each one can have the merit of responding אָמֵן many times.

בָּרוּךְ Blessed are You, HASHEM, our God, King of the universe, Who gave the heart understanding[1] to distinguish between day and night.

בָּרוּךְ Blessed are You, HASHEM, our God, King of the universe, Who did not make me a non-Jew.

בָּרוּךְ Blessed are You, HASHEM, our God, King of the universe, Who did not make me a slave.

Men say:	Women say:
בָּרוּךְ Blessed are You, HASHEM, our God, King of the universe, Who did not make me a woman.	בָּרוּךְ Blessed are You, HASHEM, our God, King of the universe, Who made me according to His will.

בָּרוּךְ Blessed are You, HASHEM, our God, King of the universe, Who gives sight to the blind.[2]

בָּרוּךְ Blessed are You, HASHEM, our God, King of the universe, Who clothes the naked.

בָּרוּךְ Blessed are You, HASHEM, our God, King of the universe, Who releases the bound.[3]

בָּרוּךְ Blessed are You, HASHEM, our God, King of the universe, Who straightens the bent.[2]

בָּרוּךְ Blessed are You, HASHEM, our God, King of the universe, Who spreads out the earth upon the waters.[4]

Nusach Sefard reverses the order of the following two blessings.

בָּרוּךְ Blessed are You, HASHEM, our God, King of the universe, Who has provided me my every need.

בָּרוּךְ Blessed are You, HASHEM, our God, King of the universe, Who firms man's footsteps.[5]

(1) Cf. *Iyov* 38:36. (2) *Tehillim* 146:8. (3) V. 7. (4) Cf. *Tehillim* 136:6. (5) Cf. 37:23.

[147] ARISE AND SING

בָּרוּךְ אַתָּה יהוה אֱלֹהֵינוּ מֶלֶךְ הָעוֹלָם, אוֹזֵר יִשְׂרָאֵל בִּגְבוּרָה.

בָּרוּךְ אַתָּה יהוה אֱלֹהֵינוּ מֶלֶךְ הָעוֹלָם, עוֹטֵר יִשְׂרָאֵל בְּתִפְאָרָה.

בָּרוּךְ אַתָּה יהוה אֱלֹהֵינוּ מֶלֶךְ הָעוֹלָם, הַנּוֹתֵן לַיָּעֵף כֹּחַ.[1]

Although many *siddurim* begin a new paragraph at וִיהִי רָצוֹן, the following is one long blessing that ends at לְעַמּוֹ יִשְׂרָאֵל.

בָּרוּךְ אַתָּה יהוה אֱלֹהֵינוּ מֶלֶךְ הָעוֹלָם, הַמַּעֲבִיר שֵׁנָה מֵעֵינָי וּתְנוּמָה מֵעַפְעַפָּי. וִיהִי רָצוֹן מִלְּפָנֶיךָ, יהוה אֱלֹהֵינוּ וֵאלֹהֵי אֲבוֹתֵינוּ, שֶׁתַּרְגִּילֵנוּ בְּתוֹרָתֶךָ וְדַבְּקֵנוּ בְּמִצְוֹתֶיךָ, וְאַל תְּבִיאֵנוּ לֹא לִידֵי חֵטְא, וְלֹא לִידֵי עֲבֵרָה וְעָוֹן, וְלֹא לִידֵי נִסָּיוֹן, וְלֹא לִידֵי בִזָּיוֹן, וְאַל [תַּשְׁלֶט] (יִשְׁלֹט) בָּנוּ יֵצֶר הָרָע. וְהַרְחִיקֵנוּ מֵאָדָם רָע וּמֵחָבֵר רָע. וְדַבְּקֵנוּ בְּיֵצֶר הַטּוֹב וּבְמַעֲשִׂים טוֹבִים, וְכוֹף אֶת יִצְרֵנוּ לְהִשְׁתַּעְבֶּד לָךְ. וּתְנֵנוּ הַיּוֹם וּבְכָל יוֹם לְחֵן וּלְחֶסֶד וּלְרַחֲמִים בְּעֵינֶיךָ וּבְעֵינֵי כָל רוֹאֵינוּ, וְתִגְמְלֵנוּ חֲסָדִים טוֹבִים. בָּרוּךְ אַתָּה יהוה, גּוֹמֵל חֲסָדִים טוֹבִים לְעַמּוֹ יִשְׂרָאֵל.

בָּרוּךְ *Blessed are You, HASHEM, our God, King of the universe, Who girds Israel with strength.*

בָּרוּךְ *Blessed are You, HASHEM, our God, King of the universe, Who crowns Israel with splendor.*

בָּרוּךְ *Blessed are You, HASHEM, our God, King of the universe, Who gives strength to the weary.*[1]

Although many *siddurim* begin a new paragraph at וִיהִי רָצוֹן, *"And may it be Your will,"* the following is one long blessing that ends at לְעַמּוֹ יִשְׂרָאֵל, *". . . to His people Israel."*

בָּרוּךְ *Blessed are You, HASHEM, our God, King of the universe, Who removes sleep from my eyes and slumber from my eyelids. And may it be Your will, HASHEM, our God, and the God of our forefathers, that You accustom us to [study] Your Torah and attach us to Your commandments. Do not bring us into the power of error, nor into the power of transgression and sin, nor into the power of challenge, nor into the power of scorn. Let not the evil inclination dominate us. Distance us from an evil person and an evil companion. Attach us to the good inclination and to good deeds and force our evil inclination to be subservient to You. Grant us today and every day grace, kindness, and mercy in Your eyes and in the eyes of all who see us, and bestow beneficent kindnesses upon us. Blessed are You, HASHEM, Who bestows beneficent kindnesses upon His people Israel.*

---

(1) *Yeshayah* 40:29.

This volume is part of
THE ARTSCROLL® SERIES
an ongoing project of
translations, commentaries and expositions on
Scripture, Mishnah, Talmud, Midrash, Halachah,
liturgy, history, the classic Rabbinic writings,
biographies and thought.

For a brochure of current publications
visit your local Hebrew bookseller
or contact the publisher:

Mesorah Publications, ltd

313 Regina Avenue
Rahway, New Jersey 07065
(718) 921-9000
www.artscroll.com